singing express

Discovering the singer in every child

BOOK

GILLYANNE KAYES AND **ANA SANDERSON**
with Maureen Hanke and Helen MacGregor

Presented by Rosemary Amoani, Kim Chandler,
Nigel Pilkington, Bridgitta Roy, Kaz Simmons
and Cleveland Watkiss

Illustrations by Christiane Engel
Design by Jocelyn Lucas
Sound and film by Stephen Chadwick and Walk Tall Media

Foreword by Professor Graham Welch

A&C BLACK · LONDON

CONTENTS

First published 2010 by A&C Black Publishers Ltd
36 Soho Square
London W1D 3QY
© 2010

ISBN 978 1 4081 1513 8 (single-user licence)
ISBN 9781 4081 1512 1 (site licence)

Printed in Great Britain by Caligraving Ltd, Thetford, Norfolk

Text © 2010 Ana Sanderson and Gillyanne Kayes
Additional text by Maureen Hanke and Helen MacGregor © A&C Black
Illustrations © 2010 Christiane Engel
Sound recording and film © 2010 A&C Black
Cover illustration by James Watson

Edited and developed by Sheena Roberts
Designed by Jocelyn Lucas
Sound engineering by Stephen Chadwick
Film and film stills by Walk Tall Media

Foreword

'This volume for ages 6-7 in the **Singing Express** series is focussed on ensuring that children have systematic opportunities to explore and develop their voices within a nurturing framework that is matched to their curiosity and emergent skills. The design draws on the latest research into children's singing development to ensure that its core activities are focussed on vocal creativity, exploration, early repertoire building and the maintenance of underlying vocal health, both physically and psychologically. Care has been taken by the **Singing Express** authors to suggest practical ideas that are suitable for young children and also their teachers. There are lots of opportunities for co-investigation and exploration, for imagination, play and enjoyment. Although centred on musical ideas, the activities draw on many other parts of the curriculum and will enable children to develop their linguistic, physical and social skills, as well as increase their understanding of the world around them. Overall, this is an impressive resource and a wonderful way to promote singing development. There should be at least one copy in every school.'

Professor Graham F Welch, PhD
Chair of Music Education, Institute of Education, UL

Introduction

Gillyanne Kayes

Singing is about expression, music and voice – and the more skilled we are at using our singing voices, the more expressive we can be.

But what does more skilled mean in relation to teaching children? How, when and where can skill be developed, when there are so many other demands in the curriculum?

Singing Express offers a complete scheme for singing in the primary school: it explains how children's voices develop through childhood; provides the materials to support them with good singing experiences; and it shows how to embed singing in the school day. This can all lead to a happy singing experience in school and, ultimately, for life.

Singing Express is underpinned by
- an understanding of the child's developing voice
- how children learn in singing
- good material for exploring and developing their voices
- five key vocal learning areas
- achievable instructions
- tools for monitoring progress
- realistic examples of when and where to sing

The child's voice and how it develops

A child's voice is not the same as an adult's – a child's physical-vocal instrument is smaller:
- the lungs are smaller;
- the voice box (larynx) is smaller and in a higher position inside the neck;
- the 'texture' of the vocal fold layers is different.
  This means that:
- the pitch range is smaller than an adult's;
- there is less control over pitch in singing than in speaking;
- there is less control over breath, which makes long phrases harder to sing;
- there is less differentiation between the vowel colours;
- the register changes (vocal gear changes in the range) are in a different place.

How children learn in singing

What can they learn at this age?

Generally speaking, children between the ages of 5 and 7 do not have the fine muscular control to learn singing 'technique'. In Western culture, where we are strongly geared towards literacy, language skills are more highly developed in young children than melodic skills. Most will tend to learn and memorise words easily and melody less easily. They need singing material that enables them to experience melody and language separately, and also allows them to explore their voice as a singing instrument. The material in **Singing Express** has been created exactly for this purpose, with games, chants, vocal play, improvisations, vocables, explorations - as well as songs.

Individual children may be at one of roughly four stages of learning to sing in tune at age 5 (see p62) – with many being at stage one. In a class you can expect them to be at all different stages, which is why **Singing Express** contains a variety of singing material so that all children at all stages can participate in and enjoy singing.

By age 11 a higher percentage of children will be singing in tune, even without intervention ~ conversely, the unselfconscious enthusiasm they have often demonstrated at age 5 may have declined. **Singing Express 3-6** offers help by encouraging positive habits and positive attitudes to singing and by including everybody.

At all stages, **Singing Express** offers opportunities to explore the voice, to gain awareness and skill and to have fun.

Singing Express 2 materials

Activities, games, explorations, chants, rhymes, rap, invented tunes, stories – and songs – are all included here. They are organised into six popular themes for ages 6–7 and further suggestions are given for integrating items into specific curriculum subjects.

Singing Express 2 does not require music-reading. Easy access to the materials is gained through the extensive audio and movie demonstrations, performances and backings. The **Singing Express** website offers further support including a HELP area and sample lessons plans.

The material is set out so that you and the children can learn together about the skills required for singing, aided by the book, audio and movies. Include the children in helping to lead and demonstrate - this is a journey of exploration you can make together. Perhaps you have lost confidence in your own singing somewhere along the line in childhood or later; here is an opportunity to pick up again from that point.

Five key vocal learning areas

Singing Express is underpinned by five, key vocal learning areas: body balance, breath, pitch, sound shapers and expression. These are identified in each activity by the learning area heading and in the activity instructions and outcomes, showing how the material helps develop the children's vocal experience and learning.

1. BODY BALANCE

Posture is not a fixed position.

Our voice is inside our body, so a balanced and energised body is best for singing. Fun movement routines help children engage physically so that they are ready for the task of singing. In **Singing Express** we have also identified a **ready position** which is helpful when there is a need to focus on the singing learning (see page 62). When we need to be still for singing, the 'ready position' is the best and most efficient position to be in. Several of the activities help the children find the ready position for themselves. Movement can be modified to suit needs of children with less mobility, involving arms and shoulders, head, neck and trunk when seated.

2. BREATH

Where breathing happens.

Nothing happens in singing without breath! Breathing for singing is also good for life, allowing us to breathe more deeply into the lungs.

When we breathe into our middles, breath comes more deeply into the lungs. Whenever we take a breath, the tummy needs to move out; whenever we sing (breathe out), the tummy needs to pull in. This helps to squeeze the air and make the voice-box buzz (see 'Hands on tummies' p10).

Breath 'control' in singing is really to do with timing: how we time the in-breath to fit with the music and phrase; how we organise the out-breath to fit with the music and phrase. Breathing patterns for singing tend to be different from those in speech because in singing the pitch (note) is often elongated.

3. PITCH

Pitch is vibration or a 'buzz' – when your voice-box buzzes it makes the pitch or note.

Every child can do a pitch glide (see 'Puppet on a string' p8) and that means they can make notes. Singing 'in tune' (getting the right note) requires experimentation and practice. In **Singing Express** we make a distinction between two areas of learning needed for pitching: pitch exploration and pitch-matching.

- **pitch exploration**: through pitch exploration the children can enjoy their full vocal range: speaking in low growly voices, high squeaky voices and exploring direction of pitch using pitch glides (see 'Monti in space' p28 and 'Deep in the deep' p52). In general, when learning to pitch, big movements are easier to do than smaller ones at first. Through opportunities to 'sing up high' and 'sing down low' the children find and e-xperience the shape of pitch as it moves about.

- **pitch-matching**: through pitch-matching the children can develop conscious control of pitch within a smaller range of notes that will be comfortable for any child to sing. **Singing Express 2** songs fall within this comfortable pitch range making them ideal for practising and learning pitch-matching.

Through opportunities to sing learned songs on higher and lower starting notes (see 'I'm so hot' p50 and 'The hungry rabbit' p22) children can still experiment with their range while also pitch-matching.

4. SOUND SHAPERS

Our mouths, jaw and lips shape the sound.

The tube of our voice is like any other tube – if we blow or talk through it the sound will change or 'resonate'. Our sound shapers also play in important part in articulating vowels and consonants, essential in language skills. We can use the same vowels and pronunciation for singing that we use to speak.

5. EXPRESSION

Every song tells a story or makes a mood.

We sing for many reasons – to express ourselves and our feelings, to tell or remember a story, to create a mood. Sub elements in expression are sound effects, tone of voice and volume. Communicative sub elements of expression are ownership (making the song your own by adding verses, characters or topics) and story-telling. Sound effects enable us to explore our voices separately from formal language, so that we can experience our voice as a unique 'noise maker'. For **Singing Express 2** the emphasis is on exploration. In later stages of **Singing Express** we explore different voice colours in a more structured way.

Monitoring progress

Teaching tip boxes touch on specifics for monitoring progress and there is further guidance on page 62 of this book and in the HELP area of the **Singing Express** website.

Where and when, getting started, moving on

In the notes at the start of each theme and under the 'Where and when' headings on the page, you will find helpful suggestions for how to integrate the activities into other subjects and where in the school you might use them.

Each item offers suggestions for 'Getting started' and for 'Moving on'. These ways in and through the material are for you to take and modify to suit your own individual teaching methods and situations.

Singing Express Songbooks

The **Singing Express** scheme is supported by a separately available, complete set of songbooks for music readers. These contain the songs from the associated **Singing Express** pack in staff notation with piano accompaniments and guitar chords and a CD of song performance tracks.

using the singing express pack

THE DVD-ROM ~ a digital copy of the book

The **Singing Express 2** DVD-ROM contains a digital copy of this book in a format suitable for display on a computer screen or whiteboard. The digital copy is in pdf format and opens in Acrobat Reader (version 6 or later). (If Acrobat Reader is not installed on your computer, you will need to download and install the appropriate version for your computer in order to open the pdf.)

The DVD-ROM window which opens on launch, contains a START pdf, from which you can navigate to any part of the **Singing Express 2** content.

The pdf page for each activity (see sample below) contains embedded audio and movie files and extra whiteboard displays accessed by clicking on the associated icon. When a movie icon is selected, the movie opens (and can be closed) within the document. It has controls for play, pause, fast forward and back, etc. When an audio icon is selected, a small player window opens, giving you controls as above. In addition some of the movies have a drop down menu (to the right of the progress bar) which enables you to select individual verses of songs.

THE DVD-ROM ~ audio and movie files

Also on the DVD-ROM are located all the source files for the embedded movies and audio. You can open these directly – instead of through the activity pdf. Simply click on the file and your computer's default media player will launch the movie or audio. A chart of all the audio and movie file names is on page 64.

QUICKTIME AV CONTROLS

There are some advantages in selecting Quicktime as the player for opening the audio files directly from the DVD-ROM. Quicktime has a feature called AV (audio visual) Controls, which enables you to raise and lower the pitch, or speed up and slow down the playback. This is particularly useful for starting a song on a higher or lower note, as recommended in many activities (see 'I've got a voice' p11). Slowing up the audio may also be useful if any of the children are finding the recorded speed too challenging.

THE AUDIO CD

The **Singing Express 2** Audio CD contains all the audio performance tracks for those times when you wish to access them with a conventional CD player. The track numbers are listed on page 64.

THE SINGING EXPRESS WEBSITE

The **Singing Express** website which offers additional support including a HELP area, can be launched from the DVD-ROM by selecting the link located on each page, or by going to www.singingexpress.co.uk

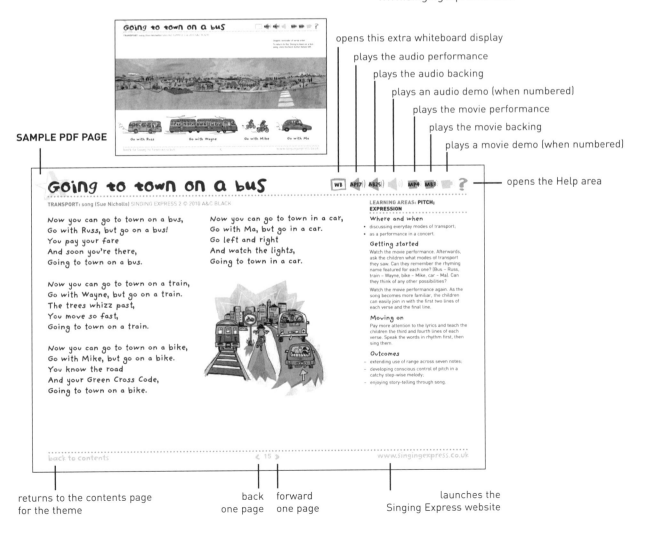

opens this extra whiteboard display
plays the audio performance
plays the audio backing
plays an audio demo (when numbered)
plays the movie performance
plays the movie backing
plays a movie demo (when numbered)

opens the Help area

SAMPLE PDF PAGE

returns to the contents page for the theme

back one page

forward one page

launches the Singing Express website

one thing I like

AP6)) AB10)))) MP1 MB1 ?

If there's one thing I like,
One thing I really like,
    Riding my bike is the top.
    I could ride all the morning,
    Ride all the afternoon,
Wishing my day would never stop.

If there's one think I like,
One thing I really like,
    Kicking my ball is the top.
    I could kick all the morning,
    Kick all the afternoon,
Wishing my day would never stop.

If there's one thing I like,
One thing I really like,
    Reading my book is the top.
    I could read all the morning,
    Read all the afternoon,
Wishing my day would never stop.

If there's one thing I like,
One thing I really like,
    Eating ice-cream is the top.
    I could eat all the morning,
    Eat all the afternoon,
Wishing my day would never stop.

LEARNING AREAS: BREATH; PITCH

Where and when

- in a PHSE discussion about activities we do with others and those we do by ourselves;
- as part of a concert programme.

Getting started

This is a song for enjoying and singing out.

Listen to the audio or movie performance. When the first two lines and the last become familiar, join in – they are the same in each verse. Notice that the last line is more extended than the others. Practise making the word 'day' long and sustained.

Then learn the middle section.

Moving on

When the song is familiar, sing along with the movie backing.

Ask the children what they really like doing. Can any of their ideas be made into new verses?

Outcomes

- learning conscious control of smaller steps in pitch-matching;
- increasing flexibility in breath use with short and long phrases;
- developing sense of tune or melody as part of song.

TEACHING TIPS
Encourage the children to use the ready position when singing the song. This will help with their breathing and ability to focus on the tune as well as the words, and increase their enjoyment.

Food

ENERGISER

This fun action game will get the children energised at the beginning of a singing session or whenever you want. Change the order of the beans to keep the children focussed. When the children know it they will want to play it themselves in the playground, taking it in turns to be the leader.

LEARNING AREAS: **PITCH**

An energising action song with a short, repetitive melody, which is excellent for **pitch-matching** practice. The actions develop co-ordination and rhythm skills and the children will have fun trying out their own action words and making up a matching dance sequence in PE, indoors or out.

LEARNING AREAS: **BODY BALANCE; PITCH**

A lively call and response game song with actions which encourage awareness of the body to help find the **ready position** for singing. A good starter for a singing session in class or assembly.

LEARNING AREAS: **BREATH; SOUND SHAPERS**

This investigation helps children to understand about the link between **breath** and the length of a vocal sound; it also invites them to think about the way sound changes in different environments. Combine it with science work about how sounds are produced.

LEARNING AREAS: **BREATH; PITCH**

A simple song with a five-note melody exploring links between breath and **pitched** sound. Use it as a warm up for a dance session by making up a sequence of movements which express the 'fizz ~ pop' lyrics.

LEARNING AREAS: **BREATH; PITCH; SOUND SHAPERS**

A lively song with rhythmic vocal patterns. Use this song in circle time to discuss favourite foods. Combine with phonics work to explore the phonemes 'ch', 's', 'p'.

LEARNING AREAS: **PITCH; EXPRESSION**

A familiar tune ('There was a princess long ago') with funny new words about likes and dislikes. Use it to stimulate inventing more yucky verses. An ideal activity for a PHSE session discussing similarities and differences.

LEARNING AREAS: **BREATH; PITCH**

A song which tells a story using the same melody as the previous activity. Ask the children to add actions to reinforce the sense of sequence. Explore the repeating rhyming words in literacy.

LEARNING AREAS: **PITCH; SOUND SHAPERS**

This tongue-twister, revolting recipe song has lovely alliterative vocabulary to enjoy and which helps improve articulation, by working the **sound shapers**. Provide children who find it hard to memorise the words with plenty of opportunities to sing and say short phrases taken from each line, eg 'chunky chicory'.

LEARNING AREAS: **PITCH**

Like 'Hungry rabbit' this song has a familiar tune ('Pop goes the weasel') with a new set of words. Many children will know the tune already and will enjoy focussing on the lyrics and noticing the alliteration. Use the song to introduce a discussion or survey of the different foods we eat at meal times.

LEARNING AREAS: **SOUND SHAPERS; EXPRESSION**

Recap the story of the magic porridge pot, then perform this echo chant with the children copying each phrase. Hearing you (or the audio presenter) using your voice with **expression** will encourage them to explore their own voices. When they know the chant well, let individual children lead the class.

LEARNING AREAS: **PITCH**

A celebratory song about food from different cultures. Watch the movie to see the foods being prepared and help the children learn the words. A wonderful song to use in cross-curricular work or to celebrate different cultures in your school community.

Sing it at an international event and cook up the recipes for everyone to taste.

See page 62 for information on emboldened words or go to HELP at www.singingexpress.co.uk

busy beans

FOOD: action game (traditional)

Jumping beans	(jump up and down)
Jelly beans	(wobble about)
String beans	(skip with a pretend skipping rope)
Butter beans	(butter your toast)
Chilli beans	(shiver and rub arms)
Broad beans	(stretch arms out wide)
Runner beans	(run on the spot)
French beans.	**Ooh la la!**

ENERGISER

Where and when

- at any time to focus the children's attention;
- as a warm up for PE – indoors or out;
- as a wet playtime game.

Getting started

Familiarise the children with the action for each bean then check their memories by pointing to a bean on the whiteboard display – the children respond with the action. Ask a confident child to lead the activity.

Play the game listening to the audio demo. There is a gap for each action.

Moving on

Using the audio backing, lead the activity, but change the order of the beans – the children have to respond to the words they hear.

Outcomes

- engaging the body in an energised way;
- responding with movement to cues.

The banana song

FOOD: action song (traditional)

Peel banana, peel peel banana,
Peel banana, peel peel banana.

Slice banana, slice slice banana,
Slice banana, slice slice banana.

Mash banana, mash mash banana,
Mash banana, mash mash banana.

Lick banana, lick lick banana,
Lick banana, lick lick banana.

Eat banana, eat eat banana,
Eat banana, eat eat banana.

Go bananas, go go bananas,
Go bananas, go go bananas.

BANANA SPLIT!

LEARNING AREAS: PITCH

Where and when

- in a literacy lesson exploring 'ee', 'i...e', 'sh', 'ck', 'ea' phonemes;
- in science or PHSE work on healthy eating;
- in dance to create movement sequences.

Getting started

Watch the movie demo and join in with the actions.

Moving on

Learn the simple three-note melody then practise the song without the backing. Try out different starting notes so that the children practise it in different keys. This will help develop their pitch-matching skills.

Put the song and actions together. There are many versions of this traditional song. Make up your own by substituting the first word with any doing word (verb) of your choice, together with an action, eg 'jump banana', 'bike banana', 'ski banana', etc.

Outcomes

- gaining confidence in pitch-matching;
- developing a sense of rhythm and physical co-ordination;
- being creative with words and actions.

chicken in a tractor

TRANSPORT: song-chant (AS)

Sing: Chicken in a tractor ~ chugga chugga chug
       Chicken in a tractor ~ chugga chugga chug

Chant: 'Cluck cluck cluck,' we heard him shout!
        'Cluck cluck cluck, can you get me out?'

Cow in a motorcar ~ vrm vrm vrm
Cow in a motorcar ~ vrm vrm vrm
'Moo moo moo,' we heard him shout!
'Moo moo moo, can you get me out?'

Pig in a plane ~ nyeeow...
'Oink oink oink...'

Sheep in a ship ~ splish splash splosh...
'Baa baa baa...'

Horse in a helicopter ~ flicker flacker flick...
'Neigh neigh neigh...'

ENERGISER

Where and when
- as part of PHSE, talking about songs which make us laugh and feel happy;
- in literacy or drama, creating a story around the animals in the vehicles.

Getting started
Listen to the audio performance. As the chanted animal sound effects become familiar, join in with them. Make them energised and fun. Learn the whole of lines 3 and 4 which are chanted.

Learn the sung lines (1 and 2). The melody is the same as the beginning of 'Skip to my lou', and contains jumps. Begin by joining in with the transport sound effect, then sing both lines.

Moving on
Can the children invent their own verses with new animals, modes of transport and sounds for them?

Watch the movie demo together to learn the optional clapping pattern.

Outcomes
- feeling energised and coordinated.

Rocket rhyme

MD8 ?

TRANSPORT: movement activity (AS)

10 9 8 7 6 5 4 3 2 1 ~

Blast off! (be a rocket blasting off)

Gravity zero! (float)

Back to earth. (land)

Ready to sing. (find ready position)

LEARNING AREAS: BODY BALANCE

Where and when
- as a preparation for a singing session;
- exploring body weight and balance in PE.

Getting started
Remind the children about the ready position. Help them to find their ready position using the information and chant, 'Ready to sing' and 'Shippety shore' (pp8-9).

Moving on
Watch the 'Rocket rhyme' movie performance and copy the presenter's movements.

Outcomes
- using guided movements and imagination to find out about the ready position.

TEACHING TIPS
Notice which children follow the presenter's movements easily and which seem to have difficulty? Are they able to stand easily in the ready position at the end of the rhyme?

Sounds like a Spacemouse

TRANSPORT: activity (based on Monti in space by Kirsty Young)

LEARNING AREAS: PITCH

Where and when

- in circle time, practising communication and leadership skills by conducting the class;
- as a way of revising pitch in a music session.

Getting started

Watch the movie demo of Monti's sirening sound – a technique for pitch gliding across the range of the voice. The sound is made first by a female voice, then echoed by a male voice. Notice how the presenter conducts the up and down vocal glides with a corresponding hand movement.

Moving on

All conduct and make the sounds for each attempt that Monti makes to get higher (you may like to use the whiteboard display). Help find Monti's sirening voice by quietly saying 'ng' on a high pitch (lips can be open or closed).

Outcomes

- exploration of full vocal range using sirening;
- learning about direction in pitch.

Monti in Space

TRANSPORT: story (Kirsty Young)

Monti was a small mouse with a tiny voice. This is the sound Monti made:

(conduct and make Monti's 'ng' sound)

You make Monti's tiny sound. (All make Monti's 'ng' sound.)
Monti was only a small mouse, but he had a big dream. He wished he could fly to the stars. But the stars were very high up. How would he ever reach them?

Monti decided that he would try to climb as high as possible. First he climbed up a lamp-post. Here's Monti climbing up the lamp-post:

(conduct and make Monti's 'ng' as though creeping up a lamp-post. The children copy the movement and echo with their voices.)

LEARNING AREAS: PITCH

Where and when

- at a participatory storytime;
- as a way in to measuring distance/height.

Getting started

Remind the children of Monti's sound and how you conducted the sound with your hand.

Moving on

Tell the story, and make and conduct the sound effects. Invite individuals to conduct Monti's movements.

Invite the children to think of other ways in which Monti might try to reach the stars – what sound would he make?

Outcomes

- learning about direction of pitch through sirening and conducting;
- exploring the individual's full vocal range with pitch glides.

TEACHING TIPS
Help the children to find their Monti sound by asking them to elongate the 'ng' at the end of the word 'sing'. It does not matter if at the end of the sound the children make a hard 'g'.

TRANSPORT: story (Kirsty Young)

But the lamp-post wasn't nearly high enough, so Monti slid down again. (Conduct a quick 'ng' slide down.)

Next, Monti went to the highest building he could see and took the lift right to the top floor. (Long 'ng' slide up.) But the building wasn't nearly high enough, so Monti took the lift all the way down again. (Long 'ng' slide down.) 'Bother,' said Monti, 'I am too low to reach those stars. I need to get higher!'

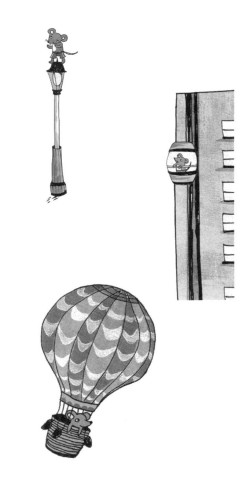

So, Monti climbed into the basket of a hot air balloon, which took him high into the air. (Long slow 'ng' slide up, floating and rising from side to side.) He was now a very long way from the ground, so his little voice sounded really small. But the balloon didn't go high enough either, and soon Monti was floating back down to the ground again. (Long slow 'ng' slide down, floating and descending from side to side.)

Monti even took a ski lift to the top of a very high mountain, which reached even higher than the clouds, to see if he could reach the stars. (Start low and go higher and higher on 'ng'.) But even from the very top of the tallest mountain, he couldn't reach the stars. So Monti skied down the mountain, right to the bottom again. (Start high and make fast, descending 'ng'.)

'I'm never going to reach the stars,' Monti sighed. 'I've climbed a lamp-post, and slid down.' (Repeat lamp-post 'ng' up and down.) 'I've gone up in a lift to the top of a building and come down.' (Repeat lift 'ng' up and down.) 'I've sailed into the sky in a hot air balloon, and floated down.' (Repeat balloon 'ng' up and down.) 'And I've gone to the top of a mountain and skied down!' (Repeat ski lift and skiing 'ng' up and down.)

Monti suddenly knew what he really needed. He wrote a nice letter to the captain of the famous space shuttle. 'We've never had a mouse on board before,' said the captain. 'You can be our first!'

The space shuttle flew Monti high into the sky, beyond the clouds, and into space, where the stars shone brightly. At last, Monti had reached the stars.

TEACHING TIPS

Monti's story helps with our understanding of 'up' and 'down' in pitch. Notice which children seem to follow the physical up and down movements easily with their voices; are any of them having difficulty with this? Which children seem most in control of big pitch glides; small pitch glides? (See p62.) Remember that the siren is a quiet sound. If the children get too loud, remind them how small Monti Mouse is and that he doesn't make a loud sound.

Growth and change

See page 62 for information on emboldened words or go to HELP at www.singingexpress.co.uk

wellies

GROWTH AND CHANGE: action chant (Val and David Machell)

Wellies in the puddle with a splish splish splish,

(splash in a puddle)

Kicking up the leaves with a swish swish swish,

(kick up leaves)

Branches all a-blowin', it's a windy day,

(arms are blown about)

Out comes the sun and it's time to play.

(stretch arms up and out for the sun, then wave as though cheering)

AB26 AD9

ENERGISER

Where and when

- lining up on the way out to play or in the playground;
- in a science lesson about weather and seasons.

Getting started

Have fun exploring and doing the actions that go with the chant. Make the movements energised.

Moving on

As the children listen to the audio demo, they do the actions. As the chant becomes more familiar, join in with the words as well. Enjoy chanting the 'splish' and 'swish' words.

Outcomes

- feeling physically energised and alert.

Tall as a tree

GROWTH AND CHANGE: action rhyme (AS)

(Begin by standing with feet together)

Stand tall as a tree ~

(stand tall)

Plant your roots in the ground ~

(lift and place each foot, feeling the ground)

Sway in the breeze ~

(sway from side to side)

But don't make a sound ~

(continue swaying)

Grow your branches ~

(slowly start stretching arms up...

Wide and strong ~

(...and stretch arms out wide and lower)

Stand tall as a tree ~

(stand tall and find ready position)

Now we're ready for a song ~

(stand in ready position)

MD11

LEARNING AREAS: BODY BALANCE

Where and when

- to warm up before class or assembly singing;
- before a performance.

Getting started

Ask the children to pretend to be tall trees. Where are their roots/their trunk/their branches? How will they move in a gentle breeze/stronger wind/force ten gale?

Moving on

Watch the movie demo and join in with the actions, which are gentle and calm.

The rhyme helps children perform a sequence of gentle movements before finding their ready position. The aim of the ready position is to find stillness and balance rather than stiffness. The sequence of movements will help the children to find these.

Outcomes

- learning about the ready position;
- exploring body balance through guided movements.

TEACHING TIPS

Use this rhyme before performing a song to focus the children's attention and concentration ready for singing and to create a communal sense of calm.

song of the tree

AP18 AB27

Big tall trees in the forest grow,

(stand tall)

Way-oh-nah-noo-day-oh,

Burying their roots in the ground below,

(feel the ground with your feet)

Way-oh-nah-noo-no.

Big strong branches stretched out wide,

(make arms into branches)

Way-oh-nah-noo-day-oh,

Blowing and swaying from side to side,

(sway gently from side to side)

Way-oh-nah-noo-no.

Bare in the winter cold and snow,

(spiky fingers)

Buds come in springtime, watch them grow,

(budding fingers)

Green summer leaves turn to autumn gold,

(leafy hands stretching out)

See them swirling, whirling, twirling down.

(leafy hands flutter down)

LEARNING AREAS: BODY BALANCE; PITCH; EXPRESSION

Where and when

- in science work on plant life cycles;
- in dance to explore shapes and qualities of movement.

Getting started

Listen to the audio performance and join in with the actions. The first section movements relate to ready position; the second has finger and hand movements.

Join in with the 'Way-oh...' lines.

Sing the first section of the song and remind the children to find their ready position. The gentle swaying movement will help release any stiffness.

Moving on

The second section ('Bare in the winter...') tells the story of the tree's growth cycle. The final phrase of the song climbs up and then down through a seven-note pitch range. Enjoy the 'swirling', 'twirling', 'whirling' words on this melody pattern.

Outcomes

- embedding the idea of body balance with actions as part of the song narrative;
- managing the voice in a seven-note melody.

TEACHING TIPS
Let the children explore the different feel or mood of the narrative parts of the song. How does the music of the song make them feel?

SPLASH

WATER: energiser (Stephen Chadwick)

Come on, come on, come on, come on SWIM,
Come on, come on, come on, come on SWIM,
Come on, come on, come on, come on SWIM,
Let's all go and SWIM.

Come on, come on, come on, come on DIVE...

Make a ripple, make a splash,
Ride a wave and dash, dash, dash!
In the sea or in the pool,
Water sports are really cool!

Come on, come on, come on, come on ROW...

Come on, come on, come on, come on SAIL...

Make a ripple, make a splash...

ENERGISER

Where and when
- as an energiser to start the afternoon;
- as part of discussing exercise.

Getting started
Ask everyone to think of a water sport they know (swimming, diving, rowing, canoeing, sailing, synchronised swimming...). Make up actions for each.

Play a game: you call out the name of a water sport and the children act it out.

Moving on
Listen to the audio performance and use the song as an energiser:
- join in with the last word of each line of the verse ('swim', 'dive', 'row', 'sail');
- join in with actions;
- join in with the whole verse 'Come on...' with actions;
- finally, add the chorus.

Outcomes
- being physically active and imaginative;
- responding to a cue.

Ice~water~vapour

WATER: activity (AS)

LEARNING AREAS: BODY BALANCE

Where and when
- as a warm up to singing a song about water;
- talking about science and the states of water.

Getting started
Introduce the children to, or remind them of ready position (see p9 or p62).

Moving on
Prepare to play a short game. Ask the children to pretend to be like: ice (frozen still); water (rippling); vapour (floating).

You lead, calling out 'ice', 'water', 'vapour' or 'ready position', and the children respond. Notice which children are finding their ready position easily, those who are struggling, and those trying too hard.

A confident child can lead this game.

Outcomes
- finding the ready position.

washing machine

WATER: song (words Sue Nicholls, tune 'Bye baby bunting')

Slow and fast, then fast and slow,
Round and round and round you go,
Changing speeds to wash and spin,
Here's the song of our washing machine.

LEARNING AREAS: PITCH; EXPRESSION

Where and when

- part of a discussion on our environment;
- in science when talking about machines.

Getting started

Ask the children to invent vocal sound effects for a washing machine (eg filling with water, spinning slowly, spinning quickly). Listen to the sound effects on the audio or movie demo. Join in with the effects and add your own.

Moving on

Learn the song (tune 'Bye baby bunting'). Sing it unaccompanied. Begin on different starting notes, to practise pitch-matching.

Create your own washing machine performance with sound effects by singing unaccompanied or using the audio backing.

Outcomes

- practising pitch-matching in a five-note melody;
- being creative with sound;
- following cues.

rain sounds

 MD14 ?

WATER: activity (Helen MacGregor and Walk Tall Media)

Make a rain picture with your voices.

LEARNING AREAS: SOUND SHAPERS; EXPRESSION

Where and when

- in an art session on collage;
- in music, conducting sounds from a score.

Getting started

Watch the movie and ask the children to suggest vocal sounds or words for rain (eg 'drizzle', 'shhhhhh', 'drip', 'pit pit', 'splash'). Collect their ideas. Using paper, water and a range of paints, charcoal and chalks, each child creates a picture of one sound idea. Combine the pictures in a rain collage.

Moving on

Make up a piece of 'Rainy day music' using the rain collage as a score:

- point to pictures or groups of pictures to cue the children to make their sounds or words;
- ask a child to lead.

Outcomes

- exploring group sounds with a visual stimulus;
- exploring the voice as an instrument.

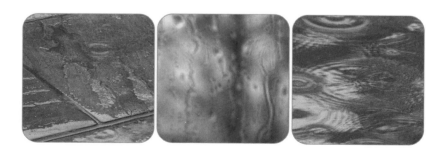

 Storm

WATER: sound effect chant (Helen MacGregor)

Hush		hush	
Splish	splash	splish	splash
Rush	dash	rush	dash
Splish	splash	splish	splash
Slish	slosh	slish	slosh
Splish	splash	splish	splash
Bash	lash	bash	lash
Splish	splash	splish	splash
CRASH		FLASH	
SPLISH	SPLASH	SPLISH	SPLASH
Bash	lash	bash	lash
Splish	splash	splish	splash
Slish	slosh	slish	slosh
Splish	splash	splish	splash
Rush	dash	rush	dash
Splish	splash	splish	splash
Hush		hush	
Splish	splash	splish	splash

Wishhhhhhhhhhhhhhhhhhhhhhhhhhhhhh

LEARNING AREAS: SOUND SHAPERS; EXPRESSION

Where and when
- in music to prepare the class for composing;
- as part of work on weather around the world;
- in literacy exploring -sh endings.

Getting started
Lead this sound picture of a storm by chanting the call lines – the children respond with the line 'splish splash splish splash'.

Begin very quietly. Get gradually louder up to the 'Crash flash' line then gradually quieter as the thunder storm passes.

Moving on
Ask the children to make up their own storm sounds. Individual children can lead using their own words and word sounds. The others respond as before with 'splish splash...'. The leader can shape the volume as she wishes.

Outcomes
- exploring 'sh' as an end sound with different vowel and consonant onsets;
- being creative with volume for expression.

Turn off that tap

WATER: song (Kaye Umansky)

Give yourself a clap ~ clap, clap, clap,
Each time you turn off that tap,
Water is for tasting, water's not for wasting,
Let's turn off that tap.
    Drip drip drip,
     Get a grip,
    Let's turn off that tap.
    Drop drop drop,
    Make it stop,
    Let's turn off that tap. YEAH!

LEARNING AREAS: BREATH; PITCH

Where and when
- learning about water as a precious resource;
- part of a movement and dance session.

Getting started
Listen to the audio performance and sing the phrases 'Let's turn off that tap' (lines 4, 7 and 10) and 'Each time you turn off that tap' (line 2). Which is longer/goes higher? ('Each time...')

Moving on
Learn the whole song. Which children are naturally taking a breath in the gaps between phrases in the second half of the song? Feeling the beat and rhythm of a song helps with the breathing.

Outcomes
- learning about breath through different phrase lengths;
- pitch-matching with steps and leaps.

Rabbits say nothing

OUR WORLD: song (Kirsty Young)

The countryside's a noisy place,
When all the animals sing.
But they all make a different sound,
Now isn't that a funny thing?

Cows say moo moo moo,
Listen to them call:
Cows say moo moo moo,
But rabbits say nothing at all, (twitch twitch)
Rabbits say nothing at all.

Horses say neigh neigh neigh,
Listen to them call:
Horses say neigh neigh neigh,
Cows say moo moo moo,
But rabbits say nothing at all, (twitch twitch)
Rabbits say nothing at all.

Cockerels say cock a doodle doo...
...Horses say neigh neigh neigh,
Cows say moo moo moo,
But rabbits say nothing at all, (twitch twitch)
Rabbits say nothing at all.

Sheep dogs say woof woof woof...
...Cockerels say cock a doodle doo,
Horses say neigh neigh neigh,
Cows say moo moo moo,
But rabbits say nothing at all. (twitch twitch)
Rabbits say nothing at all.

The countryside's a noisy place,
When all the animals sing.
But they all make a different sound,
Now isn't that a funny thing?

(CACOPHONY INTERLUDE)

We all say, 'Quiet please!
We can hear you all!'
We all say, 'Quiet please!'
THEN ~ we say nothing at all (twitch twitch)
(mouth words) we say nothing at all. (twitch twitch)

LEARNING AREAS: PITCH; EXPRESSION

Where and when
- after a farm visit;
- in music with other cumulative songs, eg 'There was an old lady who swallowed a fly'.

Getting started
This is a cumulative song. The 'cows say moo moo moo' melody pattern features strongly throughout. Focus on the punchline: 'But rabbits say nothing at all (twitch twitch)...'. Enjoy the words and make your noses twitch.

Moving on
Introduce the opening narrative section ('The countryside...'). Speak the words, then sing them with the audio performance.

Listen to the audio performance and notice the changes of mood of the different sections:

- narrative section (calm, with longer phrases);
- cacophony interlude (noisy);
- section asking for quiet (emphatic);
- punchline ending (getting quieter and into silence with mouthed words).

Once the children are confident with each section, put them all together and enjoy the contrasts.

Outcomes
- practising pitch-matching using repeated patterns in a six-note melody;
- telling a story through song.

TEACHING TIPS
Remember not everyone will be at the same stage of pitch-matching (see p62: monitoring pitch)

---

where you live

OUR WORLD: song (David Moses)

Are there tall flats where you live,
   you live, you live?
Are there tall flats where you live like
   the tall flats near me?
Do the tall flats have lifts in,
   lifts in, lifts in?
Do the tall flats have lifts in like
   the tall flats near me?

Are there houses where you live,
   you live, you live?
Are there houses where you live like
   the houses near me?
Do the houses have gardens,
   gardens, gardens,
Do the houses have gardens like
   the houses near me?

Are there farmyards where you live,
   you live, you live?
Are there farmyards where you live like
   the farmyards near me?
Do the farmyards have ducks in,
   ducks in, ducks in?
Do the farmyards have ducks in like
   the farmyards near me?

LEARNING AREAS: PITCH; EXPRESSION

Where and when

- in an environmental study of the local area;
- as part of a maths survey of children's homes.

Getting started

Display the song words on your whiteboard and listen to the audio performance of the first verse. Can the children identify which two lines have the same melody? (Lines 2 and 4 – it may take several listenings to identify them.)

Moving on

Focus on singing the verses. Point out to the children that the whole song is a sequence of questions. Speak them together. Can the children express an enquiring tone in their singing?

Outcomes

- gaining confidence with pitch-matching to a six-note melody;
- learning to pitch-match in stepwise up and down movement and in leaps;
- enjoying song as narrative.

Electricity rap

OUR WORLD: activity (AS/GK/Stephen Chadwick)

E - lec - tri - ci - ty ~
vacuum cleaner

E - lec - tri - ci - ty ~
computer

E - lec - tri - ci - ty ~
light bulb

E - lec - tri - ci - ty ~
kettle
power drill
toaster...

TEACHING TIPS
Feeling the beat and rhythm helps with breathing. Remind the children to breathe into their middles just before they sing 'Electricity'.

LEARNING AREAS: BREATH; PITCH

Where and when
- in science;
- in dance.

Getting started
Ask the children to think of appliances that require electricity to work. How many can they think of?

Moving on
Listen to the audio backing and sing along with the word 'Electricity'.

After each 'electricity' there is a gap for individual children to call out their chosen electrical appliance. Listen to the audio demo to hear how this works then use the audio backing track to accompany the activity.

Outcomes
- gaining confidence in pitch-matching with a simple two-note repeated melody;
- developing a sense of rhythm and beat;
- learning to breathe in time with the music.

Electricity

OUR WORLD: song (Stephen Chadwick)

Electricity, find it in a battery,
Flick a little switch and the current will flow.
Electricity, surging through the circuitry,
Turning into light or making things go.
   Power to electric light,
   Glowing, burning, beaming bright.

Electricity, find it in a battery...
   Power to electric car,
   Turning wheels to travel far.

Electricity, find it in a battery...
   Power to computer game,
   Blinking, buzzing, speaks its name.

Electricity, Electricity, Electricity,
Buzzzzacrakawowazummmm!

LEARNING AREAS: BREATH; PITCH

Where and when
- in a science investigation on circuits;
- in a class assembly.

Getting started
Listen to the audio performance. What three things were powered by electricity? (Light, car, computer game.)

Learn the chorus:
- speak the words slowly;
- chant the words in the rhythm they are sung;
- sing the words.

Moving on
The verse phrases are more expansive. This requires more breath. Remind the children to breathe into their middles if they appear to be running out of breath.

Outcomes
- controlling pitch in a six-note melody;
- developing breath use with short and long phrases.

Global Black Narratives for the Classroom: Britain and Europe

Rather than reserving the teaching of Black history to Black history month, Black narratives deserve to be seen and integrated into every aspect of the school curriculum. A unique yet practical resource, *Global Black Narratives* addresses this issue by providing primary teachers with a global outline of Black history, culture and life within the framework of the UK's National Curriculum.

Each topic explored in this essential book provides teachers and teaching assistants with historical, geographic and cultural context to build confidence when planning and teaching. Full lesson plans and printable worksheets are incorporated into each topic, alongside tips to build future lessons in line with the themes explored.

Volume I of this book explores the following parts:

- Part 1 examines Black Britain, a term used to refer to African and Caribbean immigrants to the United Kingdom and their descendants. Teachers will gain essential contextual knowledge and the practical skills to deliver lessons exploring many examples of Black Britain, dating as far back as the Tudor period.
- Part 2 explores Black presence in Europe, providing focused examples of Black narratives. Topics explored include Negritude, Josephine Baker, Afro-Spaniards and the Moorish occupation of Spain, Afro-Surinamese people in the Netherlands and Black presence in France.

Created by BLAM UK, this highly informative yet practical resource is an essential read for any teacher, teaching assistant or senior leader who wishes to diversify their curriculum and address issues of Black representation within their school.

BLAM UK (Black Learning Achievement and Mental Health), founded by Ife Thompson, who is a community organiser, writer, UN fellow, lawyer and an external Black History Moderator for schools across London. She has been teaching children and young people global Black history within school settings and the wider community since 2017. The BLAM UK team has worked with schools, students, teachers and teacher training providers across the UK, BLAM teaches each global Black history focusing on the collective Black experience from a Pan-African and Racial-Wellness perspective.

Global Black Narratives for the Classroom: Britain and Europe

Practical Lesson Plans, Worksheets and Activities for Ages 7–11

BLAM UK

Routledge
Taylor & Francis Group

LONDON AND NEW YORK

Part One: Black Britain

1 The history of Jungle music?

Lesson Title: The history of Jungle music?

Lesson Aims:

1. To understand the history of Jungle music and its impact.

2. To learn the following skills:

   a. Reflection
   b. Analysis
   c. Cultural awareness

National syllabus links

History: To understand the history of the British islands as a coherent, chronological narrative, from the earliest times to the present day: how people's lives have shaped this nation and how Britain has influenced and been influenced by the wider world. Understand historical concepts such as continuity and change, cause and consequence, similarity, difference and significance; use them to make connections, draw contrasts, analyse trends and frame historically valid questions; and create their own structured accounts, including written narratives and analyses. Gain historical perspectives by placing their growing knowledge into different contexts, understanding the connections between local, regional, national and international history; between cultural, economic, military, political, religious and social history; and between short- and long-term timescales.

Music: Listen, review and evaluate music across a range of historical periods, genres, styles and traditions, including the works of great composers and musicians.

To understand and explore how music is created, produced and communicated, including through the inter-related dimensions: pitch, duration, dynamics, tempo, timbre, texture, structure and appropriate musical notations.

Worksheet Colour Code: Green: 7–8 Blue: 8–9 Orange: 9–11

Further outcomes for children

Skills in reflection and listening will be sharpened through the use of group discussion and sharing ideas (working with others).

DOI: 10.4324/9781003194378-2

Cultural awareness will increase due to learning about the Black British subculture and how it was used as a tool of expression and rebellion.

The plenary

Jungle is a British music genre, defined by its fusion of Black diasporic music from across the Black Atlantic, and these included Reggae, Ragga, Rare Grooves, Hip-Hop and dance music. It was created by working-class Black youth in the early 90s. Jungle music was significant as a means of rebellion and pushback against racism and classism. As the genre progressed it became heavily gentrified, with its originators erased and forced into the margins.

Jungle origins and history (including its social context) and the music of the Black Atlantic

Jungle is a genre of dance music that was created by Black British sound engineers and reached a popularity peak in the 80s and the 90s. Whilst producers like Shy Fx and M-Beat are considered prolific in Jungle music development, its pioneers stemmed from various African diaspora genres, including reggae and dub music. Its rhythm and bassline differed from other rave- and electronic-based music genres of the time and appealed to Black youths because of this. It was characterised by exaggerated heavy Bass with low frequency as opposed to techno's high frequency and soft Bass.[1] Jungle DJs and lovers of the music are called junglists.

Origin of name Jungle music

There are many debates and versions of how this name came to be. One traces back to Jamaican dub, reggae and dancehall genres in the 1970s, which suggested that the term 'junglist' referred either to a person from Kingston, Trenchtown, also known as the 'Concrete Jungle', or a person residing in Tivoli Gardens, 'the Gardens', in Jamaica, which were leafy areas colloquially known as 'the Jungle'. The term was also considered empowering for some, as it embodied a sense of ownership and display of the term 'Jungle music', which was often used to discriminate against music of African origin.

The first documented use of the term is in a song featuring UK Jungle pioneer Rebel MC – *"Rebel got this chant alla the junglists"*.[2] Another version of the earliest possible use of the term 'Jungle' can be found in early 20th-century Jazz. The 'Jungle style' was cultivated by Jazz legend Duke Ellington in the 1920s. This style was characterised by a heavy four-beat tread in the Bass and Drums (see East St. Louis toodle-oo in the teacher's resource guide). This song clearly demonstrates low-level frequencies seen in Jungle 70 years later). Similarly, James Brown's 'In the Jungle Groove' featured Breakbeats that were sampled in Jungle tracks. Funky Drummer, one of the most famous breakbeat samples of all time, was used in Metalheadz's 'Terminator'.[3]

The junglist method of creating music is to use samples, a common form of music creation prevalent in various forms of Black music across the Black Atlantic.[4] The term 'Black Atlantic' was coined by Professor Paul Gilroy. Paul Gilroy's term showcases how Black people across the diaspora in both the New World and Europe had formed a connected identity through the fusion and exchange of Black cultures with other Black cultures across the Black Atlantic.[5]

With this new way in which Black music was becoming globalised, sampling was inspired by an eclectic re-use of previous sounds and songs being embedded into new musical composition by way of digital encoding, popular in the era of electronic dance music. Musical sampling is still popular in Hip-Hop and sound system culture.

The UK sound system culture was brought from the Caribbean to the UK. It served as a means of preservation for Black Caribbeans who were forming a uniquely Black British identity rooted in their Caribbean one. Sound system DJs would frequently integrate rare groove and soul music. This of course gave birth to the sampling technique of Jungle DJs to come; without its influence Jungle could not have existed.[6]

Jungle music's popularity grew in Britain at this time, specifically in London and Bristol where acid house music was formed.[7] The culture itself was somewhat inclusive and broke down barriers of racism and class to an extent. However, as Black DJs began to use bBreakbeats, a faster tempo and Ragga samples, many white people felt uncomfortable with the level of unapologetic Blackness. Nevertheless, it began to take on a life of its own and was an underground success popularised by pirate radio stations like Kool FM, before receiving mainstream popularity.[8]

The rise of Jungle

At its height, at least 20,000 people raved to it in London each weekend. Jungle subculture, including raves, had become largely multicultural by this point. To date, Jungle Fever is the name of the longest running Jungle rave held in Brixton, South London, first emerging in 1993.[9] Despite its seeming racial harmony, the relations between Black and white people in larger society were at odds with this idea. Ultimately, Jungle music was a Black Youth art form that served as a rebellion against racist institutions, divisive politics and classism. For context, the Brixton uprising occurred roughly ten years before its creation, and Stephen Lawrence was brutally murdered in 1993 at its height. Jungle allowed Black Youth to redefine 'Britishness' on Black terms. This was radically different from before and helped to affirm the identities and struggles amongst Black British youth.

Downfall, gentrification, and Drum and Bass

Jungle music slowly became a genre that was disassociated from its Black British roots. Despite the underground success of Jungle, the music industry and larger culture refused to acknowledge the historical and cultural roots of Jungle in its unapologetic form. As a result, the very people that created it were slowly being erased from it. White DJs were enjoying longevity and success, a privilege and right not afforded to the Black pioneers of the sound. Black people were turned away from clubs as white club owners profited from Jungle without the 'Blackness'.

In 1995 as Jungle culture began to splinter under the weight of gentrification, white DJs sought to create a more whitewashed version of Jungle, pulling back from the undeniable ragga and reggae influence in favour of a more cerebral or less Black sound.[10] The majority of tracks no longer included the sound system MCs who had been integral to the sound just a couple of years prior.

Whitewashed Jungle gave birth to Drum and Bass which was less evidently 'Black' and thus more digestible by white society.[11] Again, Black pioneers saw no profit from this; as its popularity soared well past that of Jungles, Black creators were purposely left behind and excluded.

This poses a bigger issue of theft and erasure of Black British artistry as a whole in the UK, which often occurs because Black British artists and art entrepreneurs are largely underrepresented in industry roles, including senior positions.

The genre had now been entirely gentrified. The ramifications of this meant that the music space became less inclusive, specifically for Black women in the scene.[12] Now that Black people had been pushed to the margins of their own creations, Black women had to face not only the same racism as their Black male counterparts did, but the additional barriers of sexism and misogynoir.

Influence/future

Whilst Jungle no longer exists in its original form, there are many loyalists who are part of the subculture. Its influence cannot be denied; without it, Drum and Bass, Garage, Dubstep, and

History – KS3-GCSE – The Story of Black Migrants in England in Tudor Times [online video], BBC Teach, 22 July 2020, http://youtu.be/3WsoqpDrsf4, accessed 18 April 2021.

The National Archives, 'The king provides clothes for the party', (National Archives, no date), www.nationalarchives.gov.uk/pathways/blackhistory/early_times/docs/acc_scotp101.htm, accessed 15 April 2021.

Todd J., 'Bringing the Untold Stories of Black Tudors Into the Classroom', (Oxford University, no date, 8), SSJT4_Jason-Todd__Chris_Lewis__Bringing_the_untold_stories_of_black_Tudors_into_the_classroom.pdf, accessed 17 April 2021.

Learning objective	1. To learn about Black British Tudors and their lives. To understand the history of Black people in Britain outside of the transatlantic slave trade or a servant context.
Main activities	1. Identify Black Tudors 2. PowerPoint presentation 3. Creative writing task 4. Crossword puzzle 5. 'Word Blank' worksheet
Homework	1. Title page or poster on Black Tudors, with focus on one of the prominent figures.

In-class lessons

1. Begin by asking the children what they know about Tudors, prompting them to describe who they are, what they looked like etc. (it is likely that Black Tudors do not come to mind for the children when thinking about Tudors).
2. Hand out pictures of some of the six prominent figures outlined in the teacher resource guide. Ask them if they know any of the figures; get the children to reflect on their attire and appearance and what their occupations or their status in society might have been. Proceed to explain that they are Black Tudors.
3. Present a PowerPoint which details the history of Black Britons during the Tudor period. Key points to address:

   ● Lived experiences of Black Britons at the time.
   ● The existence of Black Britons in England outside of a servitude/transatlantic slave trade context.
   ● Why have we not heard more about Black Tudors?
   ● African presence in Roman Britain (see teacher's resource guide for information) – this point is optional but effective in helping the children to understand that an African presence has existed in Britain for many years.

4. Worksheets – Figure 2.1, Figure 2.2, Figure 2.3.

7–8 year olds – Creative Writing:

● Ask the children to complete a short story in first person from the perspective of whichever prominent figure they choose (figures should be presented in the beginning of the lesson during PowerPoint, or within the pamphlet). For younger children and children across different learning capacities, adapt this to providing a few sentences on how it might have felt to be a Black Tudor at that time or ask them to draw a portrait of a prominent Black Tudor; simplify where necessary.

8–9 year olds – Fill in the Blank:

● Complete fill in the blank worksheet (Figure 2.2).

9–11 year olds – Crossword puzzle

● Children can complete a crossword puzzle, which quizzes them on what they have learned (Figure 2.3).

New words and phrases

Blackamoor

Moor

Citizen

Migrant

The plenary

Black people existed in Britain long before the slave trade and enjoyed normal lives there. Black people made contributions to Tudor Britain; some examples include contributions to music and fashion.

Further guide of future lessons:

1. Black people in Britain before the slave trade.
2. Migration of people of Africa descent in the 700s.

Name: _____

Date: _____

DIARY OF A BLACK TUDOR

WRITE A DIARY ENTRY FROM THE POINT OF VIEW
OF A FAMOUS BLACK TUDOR! THINK ABOUT
WHAT LIFE WAS LIKE IN BRITAIN AT THE TIME,
DID THEY HAVE AN EXCITING JOB? DID THEY
HAVE FAMILY? WERE THEY HAPPY, OR SAD?

Figure 2.1 Worksheet for ages 7–8

Kokoroko – Abusey Junction (Live in Brownswood Basement) [online video], Brownswood Recordings, 12 January 2018, https://youtu.be/jo7f059kJ-A, accessed 7 April 2021.

Moanin' [online video], The Joe Harriott Quintet-Topic, 11 November 2014, https://youtu.be/Cq_fpsoMGX0, accessed 7 April 2021.

Oh Daddy! [1935] [online video], Spondonman, 21 September 2014, https://youtu.be/28cSAvvGwIY, accessed 5 April 2021 (Time stamp: 10:57–11:15)

Sky News, 'Fifty years on: Read Enoch Powell divisive rivers of blood speech', (Sky News, 20 April 2018), https://news.sky.com/story/fifty-years-since-enoch-powells-rivers-of-blood-speech-11338513, accessed 6 April 2021.

Soweto Kinch, 'Holding out for a hero: Soweto Kinch on Joe Harriott', (The Guardian, 21 July 2011), www.google.com/amp/s/amp.theguardian.com/music/2011/jul/21/soweto-kinch-on-joe-harriott

Toynbee J., Tackley C., and Doffman M., *Black British Jazz: Routes, Ownership and Performance*, 1st edn., Surrey, Ashgate Publishing Company, 2014.

Turtles [online video], Flying Lotus, 24 November 2020, https://youtu.be/zwVuqMuse4U, accessed 7 April 2021.

Yussef Kamaal – Calligraphy//Brownswood Basement Session [online video], Giles Peterson, 29 December 2016, https://youtu.be/1g826StJhLk, accessed 7 April 2021.

Learning objectives	1. To understand the evolution and formation of British Jazz. 2. To understand the importance of hybridity to its existence.
Main activities	1. Introduction – What do we already know about Jazz? 2. PowerPoint and timeline 3. Listen and analyse sound clips. 4. Worksheets
Homework	Provide the children with a music piece to listen to at home, and get them to write a short music review.

In-class lessons:

1. Quiz the children on what they already know about Jazz; if responsive, encourage them to name artists and/or instruments associated with the genre.

2. Using the teachers resource guide, create a timeline which can be printed and handed out or a PowerPoint which must also contain a timeline of key British Jazz moments and artists. Present these to the children.

3. Play a range of Black British Jazz music prior to the 2000s using the teacher resources pack. In mixed-ability pairs, ask the children to think about what instruments they can hear, pausing after each track for discussion and sharing ideas.

4. Get the children to work through the relevant worksheets.

New words and phrases

Hybridity

Township

Cosmopolitanism

Apartheid

Afrofuturism – An artistic movement incorporating science fiction, technology or fantastical elements with Black culture, politics and history.
Example: Blank Panther merges the idea of a futuristic utopian city with African culture.

Calypso

Exoticism

The plenary

British Jazz in its infancy was heavily influenced by the influx of West Indian migrants who merged music styles from across the Black Atlantic. Subsequently, South African migrants would arrive and merge Township Jazz with British Jazz. The scene would plateau before experiencing a streak of popularity in the 1980s with prominent musicians such as the Jazz Warriors acting as trailblazers. Many of these young Black musicians were descendants of West Indian migrants and were using Jazz to redefine what it meant to be Black and British. Eventually this popularity waned with many Black musicians pushed to the margins of the scene. More than 25 years later, the scene would again experience mass popularity and success. Young musicians primarily from across London, and in particular South London, would usher in a new inclusive sound, entirely their own, influenced by sounds from across the Black Atlantic like their predecessors. The most recurring theme of British Jazz is hybridity, particularly in London where this concept seems inevitable given the melting pot that it is.

Further guide for future lessons:

1. Music across the Black Atlantic.
2. A history of sound system culture in Britain.

NAME:

DATE:

BLACK BRITISH JAZZ MUSIC – KEN 'SNAKEHIPS' JOHNSON

LISTEN TO THE MUSIC CLIP, NAME FIVE INSTRUMENTS THAT YOU CAN YOU HEAR!

● _____
_____

● _____
_____

● _____
_____

● _____
_____

● _____
_____

LIST THREE FACTS YOU CAN REMEMBER ABOUT KEN 'SNAKEHIPS' JOHNSON FROM THE VIDEO CLIP!

● _____
_____

● _____
_____

● _____

Figure 3.1 Worksheet for ages 7–8

Name _____   Year _____

CLAUDIA JONES

Where was Claudia Jones born ?

_____

_____

Match The Keywords

Windrush

- A system in which there is no class hierarchy. Goods are owned by everyone and shared equally.

Deportation

- A system in which there is no class hierarchy. Goods are owned by everyone and shared equally.

Communism

- A system in which there is no class hierarchy. Goods are owned by everyone and shared equally.

Figure 4.1A Worksheet for ages 7–8

Name _____   **Year** _____

CLAUDIA JONES

Fill in the blanks

Claudia Jones played a _____ role in the anti-_____ struggle in the UK, particularly in the aftermath of the _____ Notting ____ riots, founding the West Indian Gazette newspaper as campaign platform. She died suddenly at her home in _____ Road, Gospel Oak, in _____ aged _____.

- -

Racism	Key	Lisburne
Hill	1958	49

Claudia Jones Is Known to Be the 'Mother of Notting Hill Carnival'
True or False

Figure 4.1B

Name _____ **Year** _____

CLAUDIA JONES

COLOUR ME IN!

Figure 4.1C

In-class lessons:

1. PowerPoint/pamphlet: The PowerPoint and/or pamphlet should emphasise the work Moody did in London. This will allow the children to complete the travel/timeline and connect the history with local areas they might be familiar with.
2. Next, children should be provided with a blank timeline of Moody's life and a collection of London Underground and train station signs to stick to it accordingly. Children should work in groups of three to four, collaborating to complete it.
3. An easy pop quiz should then be conducted. The teacher should split the cast into two groups and read out a series of questions. In response to each, children should raise their hands if they know the answer to a question. Whoever raises their hand first gets to answer the questions. The group with the most correct answered questions should win. Perhaps the winning team could be rewarded if there is a class star chart or something of that nature.
4. Finally, children can complete the worksheets according to their ages.

Key Words/New Phrases

Imperialism – Dominating a territory through use of military force, colonisation and/or economic control.

Colonialism – Obtaining full or partial control and dominance of a territory by exploiting its resources and economy, occupying it with settlers.

Colour bar – A system which denies Black people the same rights, opportunities and facilities as white people in society.

Pan-African – The idea that all people of African descent should be unified.
Pigmentocracy – A society where **status is organised around skin colour of which the** the lightest-skinned people have the highest social status, followed by the brown-skinned, with the black-skinned

---

The plenary

Harold Moody was an intellectual dedicated to the fight for equality in Britain. Unlike his peers, he was not completely opposed to colonialism and believed that equality and colonial rule could co-exist. Although his activism did not effect the change he wanted at the time, it has been argued that his work, in part, influenced the British Black Power movement some years later.

Further guide of future lessons:

1. The fight for racial justice and civil rights in Britain before WWII.

PLACES AND SPACES: HAROLD MOODY

Match the picture to each place

The City Harold Moody arrived in when he got to Britain

JAMAICA

The Hospital where he met his wife

PECKHAM

The Hospital he worked at after university

BRISTOL

The country he was born in

KINGS COLLEGE

The place in London that he set up his first surgery

LONDON EYE HOSPITAL

BLAM

Figure 5.1 Worksheet for ages 7–9

Name: _____   Date: _____

Harold Moody

Life can be hard for migrants today, they can experience racism and unfair treatment, Moody arrived in Britain at a time when it was very hard! List some feelings relating to each of Harold Moody's experiences

Being called names whilst walking on the street	**Being made fun of because of where you come from by friends**
Travelling for hours on a ship to a country you've never been to before	**Not being allowed to work where you want to because you are not white British**

Figure 5.2 Worksheet for ages 8–9

Stuart Hall

Look at the statements below, Are they true or false? If you think they are false, write down the correct answer underneath!

Stuart Hall was born in Guyana

☐ True   ☐ False

Stuart Hall travelled to France to study

☐ True   ☐ False

Stuart Hall was frustrated with the way things were in Jamaica before he left

☐ True   ☐ False

Stuart Hall thought migrants were part of British Culture

☐ True   ☐ False

Stuart Hall enjoyed listening to rock music, as it represented his experience as a migrant

☐ True   ☐ False

Figure 6.2 Worksheet for ages 8–9

STUART HALL AND MEDIA REPRESENTATION

Stuart Hall believed that how people are shown in the media is very important.

*His ideas about this are known as the **Reception theory**.*

What does the Reception Theory say : that media texts are created with hidden messages by the producer – they are loaded with values and messages.

·Different people and viewers will understand the media in different ways, influenced by stereotypes created by the media producer that control the way we think about ourselves and others.

·Read the scenarios below and consider how they relate to Stuart Hall's **Reception theory**.

Scenario 1: You are watching TV and the only shows you can find with Black people, all the actors are either home burglars or car stealers.

What type of hidden messages about Black people is being shown to viewers of this programme?

Why is it a hidden message and how is it a stereotype ?

Using the Reception Theory explain how can this show control the way people think about Black People ?

Figure 6.3 Worksheet for ages 9–11

© 2024, *Global Black Narratives for the Classroom: Britain and Europe*, Blam UK, Routledge

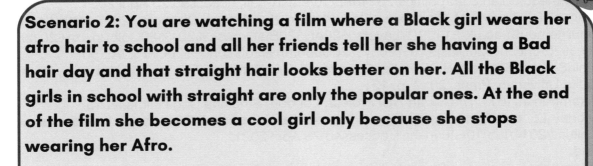

Scenario 2: You are watching a film where a Black girl wears her afro hair to school and all her friends tell her she having a Bad hair day and that straight hair looks better on her. All the Black girls in school with straight are only the popular ones. At the end of the film she becomes a cool girl only because she stops wearing her Afro.

· What hidden message about Afro hair is the producer trying to get the viewers to believe ?

· How do you think the hidden message about Afro hair will make Black girls feel ?

· What stereotypes are used in this film ?

Figure 6.3 (Continued)

Notes

1 Simkin J., 'Stuart Hall' [website], 2020, https://spartacus-educational.com/HIShallS.htm, accessed 25 April 2021.

2 Morley D., and Schwarz B., 'Stuart Hall obituary' [online], (The Guardian, 10 February 2014), www.theguardian.com/politics/2014/feb/10/stuart-hall, accessed 25 April 2021.

3 Gabriel D., *Layers of Blackness: Colourism in the African Diaspora*, 2007, http://eprints.bournemouth.ac.uk/21409/1/Layers%20of%20Blackness%20-%20Colourism%20in%20the%20African%20Diaspora%20by%20Deborah%20Gabriel%20OFFICIAL.pdf

4 Hall S., and Schwarz B., *Familiar Stranger: A Life Between Two Islands*, 1st edn., Durham, Duke University Press, 2017, p. 121.

5 Akomfrah J., (dir.), *The Stuart Hall Project*, London, Smoking Dogs Films, 2013.

6 Morley D., and Schwarz B., 'Stuart Hall obituary' [website], 2014, www.theguardian.com/politics/2014/feb/10/stuart-hall, accessed 25 April 2021.

7 Ibid.

8 Akomfrah J., (dir.), *The Stuart Hall Project*, London, Smoking Dogs Films, 2013.

9 Simkin J., 'Stuart Hall' [website], 2020, https://spartacus-educational.com/HIShallS.htm, accessed 25 April 2021.

10 Morley D., and Schwarz, B., 'Stuart Hall obituary' [website], 2014, www.theguardian.com/politics/2014/feb/10/stuart-hall, accessed 25 April 2021.

11 Simkin J., 'Stuart Hall' [website], 2020, https://spartacus-educational.com/HIShallS.htm, accessed 25 April 2021.

12 Ibid.

13 Ibid.

14 Ibid.

15 Simkin J., 'Stuart Hall' [website], 2020, https://spartacus-educational.com/HIShallS.htm, accessed 25 April 2021.

16 Morley D., and Schwarz B., 'Stuart Hall obituary' [website], 2014, www.theguardian.com/politics/2014/feb/10/stuart-hall, accessed 25 April 2021.

17 Ibid.

18 Ibid.

8 Black British publishing companies

Lesson Title: Black British publishing companies: Jessica Huntley, Eric Huntley and John La Rose

Lesson Aims:

1. To learn about independent Black British bookshops and their importance to the community
2. To learn about the work of New Beacon Books in creating supplementary schools

To learn the following skills:

1. Chronological understanding
2. Making connections between historical events
3. Critical thinking skills

National syllabus links

> **History:** To know and understand the history of the British islands as a coherent, chronological narrative, from the earliest times to the present day: how people's lives have shaped this nation and how Britain has influenced and been influenced by the wider world. Understand historical concepts such as continuity and change, cause and consequence, similarity, difference and significance; use them to make connections, draw contrasts, analyse trends and frame historically valid questions; and create their own structured accounts, including written narratives and analyses. Gain historical perspective by placing their growing knowledge into different contexts, understanding the connections between local, regional, national and international history; between cultural, economic, military, political, religious and social history; and between short- and long-term timescales.

Worksheet Colour Code: Green: 7–8 Blue: 8–9 Orange: 9–11

Further outcomes for children:

1. Chronological thinking
2. Historical comprehension
3. Analysis

Teacher resource guide

Who were Jessica and Eric Huntley?

The Huntleys were a radical activist couple. The Huntleys came from British Guyana and arrived during the height of the Windrush era in the 1950s. They exhibited an interest for politics and

DOI: 10.4324/9781003194378-9

social activism in Guyana, with Jessica leading a campaign for exploited female workers whilst just a teen.

In 1948 Jessica met Eric and married him two years later. Eric, just like Jessica, was heavily into Guyanese politics, having been a founding member of the People's Progressive Party (PPP).[1] During the same year, Jessica co-founded the Women's Progressive Organisation, which represented women's issues in the PPP's efforts towards national liberation.[2] In 1953 Eric was arrested along with his PPP peers; he was imprisoned for a year.[3] In 1957 he left for Britain to study. In the meantime, Jessica stood as a candidate for the election under the PPP. She was defeated, and thus joined her husband in England in April 1958.[4]

As soon as they arrived, they immediately became active within the British African-Caribbean community in London. Some significant campaigns which the Huntleys participated in were:

● The Community Workers Association, or CECWA – the Huntleys were founding members. It was greatly significant due to it being the very first Black education of its kind in the UK
● The Black Parents Movement – formed (with John La Rose – co-founder of New Beacon Books) as a response to the arrest of Cliff Mcdaniel, a schoolboy arrested by Haringey police outside of his school
● Anti-banding protest movement – led by the North London West Indian Association or NLWIA, the movement challenged Haringey Council's decision to segregate the learning of children according to 'bands' determined by IQ tests, which have since been discredited
● Black People's Day of Action – 20,000 Black people from across the country attended to protest
● Supplementary School Movement – designed to educate children according to the shortcomings of mainstream school, which was failing Black children[5]

The establishment of Bogle-L'Ouverture publications

In 1968 Eric and Jessica Huntley opened a bookshop in their own living room on Coldershaw Road, Ealing.[6] It was originally called 'The Bookshop',[7] and it became a hotspot for Black and migrant communities; eventually it was forced to find new premises. The Huntleys named the shop 'Bogle-L'Ouverture' (BLP). Five years later, it was renamed after Walter Rodney, a Guyanese activist who was assassinated in 1980. Before his assassination, Rodney was a radical intellectual who had been rejected entry into Jamaica and had had his writing banned in the West Indies. Many were outraged, including the Huntleys. In direct response, Bogle-L'Ouverture was born and would publish his work *The Groundings with My Brothers* in 1961,[8] as well as the groundbreaking *How Europe Underdeveloped Africa* some years later. Generally, the publications was primarily created to promote radical writing by Black people and to challenge the stereotypical and racist portrayal of Black people as written in the history books at the time.[9]

The publication company was named after two significant Caribbean freedom fighters: Paul Bogle and Toussaint L'Ouverture. The BLP began as a small self-financed bookshop, which offered an alternative radical Black perspective to the material that was available in mainstream bookshops.[10] The shop sold non-fiction, fiction, children's books and poetry. The company would eventually publish a range of notable Black British writers, which included Valerie Bloom and Linton Kwesi Johnson.[11] Due to the shop being a radical hub for African-Caribbean people and migrants, it was subject to a series of racist attacks between 1977 and 79.[12] These attacks included broken windows, vandalism, excrement put through the letterbox and calls from the Ku Klux Klan.[13] Nevertheless, Bogle-L'Ouverture stood firm, and in an alliance with New Beacon Books they did not allow themselves to be intimidated by the racist hatred.

New Beacon Books

New Beacon Books was founded by John La Rose and his partner Sarah White in 1966. It was the first Black-owned publisher and has been functioning for over 50 years. John's experiences growing up under colonialism, in both South America and the Caribbean, inspired his vision. John recognised that "colonial policy was based on a deliberate withholding of information from generation to generation. There was also a discontinuity of information from generation to generation".[14] La Rose saw publishing as a means of creating a sense of self and breaking away from this discontinuity. The company specialised in poetry, literature, non-fiction, history and children's books from African, Caribbean, Asian and African-American writers, just like Bogle-L'Ouverture.

Supplementary schools and political endeavours

Much like Bogle-L'Ouverture, New Beacon Books was also at the centre of many grassroots organisations, including, and perhaps most importantly, supplementary schools. John La Rose once said:

> Black Kids were used to hearing Africa dismissed as this primitive place. Africa is something they were a bit ashamed of. So we had to change that.[15]

In conjunction with New Beacon Books, John La Rose created a supplementary school – Albertina Sylvester School. It was originally held at 2 Albert Road, Finsbury Park – John La Rose's house.[16] In his living room, children would be taught by teachers both qualified and not, who often worked with no pay. For the majority of Black children who attended the school, this would be their first introduction to African, Caribbean, African-American and Asian history. This was because this history was not taught as part of the curriculum, and when it was, it was told from the perspective of the coloniser.[17] The school helped instil in the children high racial self-esteem. It also gave them confidence in their educational abilities, in contrast to mainstream British schools which were part of an institutionally racist system and thus told the children that they were inadequate and unintelligent as they were not white children. In addition to Saturday lessons, the school also held book fairs, stocking books about Black and Asian people and by Black and Asian people. The book fair was extremely successful. Organised with Bogle-L'Ouverture, it was known as the International Book Fair of Radical Black and Third World Books.[18] The fair ran from 1982–95.

As time progressed John La Rose and the school became increasingly involved with numerous political movements, including that of the Black Parents movement, which La Rose co-founded, in response to the brutalisation of a Black schoolboy in Haringey in 1975.[19] As a result, less attention was paid to the schools than before. In 1985 the Albertina Sylvester School became the George Padmore School,[20] named after the Pan-Africanist.

New Beacon Bookshop today

By 2016, New Beacon Bookshop had been open for 50 years, however the directors of the companies recognised that New Beacon Bookshop would not survive in the current climate (Bogle-L'Ouverture did not).The modern book industry was much different from 50 years prior.[21] Retailers such as Amazon have a wider range of books and sell them at a fraction of the price; due to this, the directors decided to close the bookshop.[22] However, a year later they decided that they would attempt to keep it open. They cultivated a group of volunteers and spread the word on social media.[23] Those who donated their time banded together and created the New Beacon Development Group to help keep New Beacon Bookshop open.[24] The community responded with a crowdfund of £12,500. This has allowed the bookshop to work towards creating ways to strive and stay open in the future.[25]

life troubles. It is also given to remain close to their parents (remain its natural environment to survive, like a fish in water).

Pepper (Ata): Pepper contains lots of seeds in its fruit – pepper is given to children so that they are have a lot of children (fruitful – children are the fruit).

Kola nut (Obi): Kola nut grows on a tree that is indigenous to West Africa.[11] When fresh, they have a bitter taste. During the ceremony, the kola nut is chewed and then spat out. It is given to repel the evil (bitterness) in life.

On some occasions, the Holy Book and/or a pen are added to the items shared with the baby by the elder.

3. Finally, the ceremony will conclude with a party. Food and music is enjoyed to celebrate the new life.

Yoruba names

Yoruba names generally and traditionally fit into categories, these include:[12]

- Destiny names (Oruko Amtorunwa): These are names which are mostly derived from religion or are consider blessed names from heaven, some examples include:

  - Taiwo and Kehinde – These are two destiny names after giving birth to twins, which is considered a blessing. The first twin would be called Taiwo and the second Kehinde.
  - Babatunde – This destiny name is given to a child born after an elder's passing.

- Acquired names (Oruko Abiso): These names are given by relatives. Some examples include:

  - Omotayo
  - Ibilola
  - Oladotun
  - Adeyinka – the prefix 'Ade' means crown and signifies a high position in society. In Nigeria 'Adeyemi' is a typical royal family name.

- Panegyrics (Oruko Oriki): These names are names which are an expression of praise, they include:

  - Ayinla
  - Ajoke
  - Alao
  - Akano

- Oriki A biku. Examples include Malomo, Kosoko, Durosinmi, Ikukoyi, Biobaku, Kokumo, Ikudaisi, Igbekoyi and Anduu.
- Christian names: Nowadays, Christian parents use traditional names but substitute Orisa (spirit/deity) for the prefix Oluwa or Olu.

  - Olu/Oluwa: Lord/my Lord. An example of this is:
  - Oluwáṣeun: The Lord has made it – the parents received the child they had prayed to God for.

- Muslim names: Muslim parents often give their children Arabic names whilst using Yoruba phonetics. Some examples include:

  - Rafiah
  - Rafiatu

The ceremonies in the UK

Yoruba naming ceremonies are an important Yoruba tradition that is continued within the Yoruba diaspora within the UK. It is normally an event that takes place in family homes with prayers and supporting friends and family in attendance. The ceremony detailed earlier is performed and the mood is one of joy, reflection and celebrations. There will be loads of foods and snacks at the end of the celebration too. With the Yoruba diaspora practising this ceremony in the UK, there has been an expansion in the way these naming ceremonies are conducted in the UK. Many younger Black-British Yorubas are opting to turn the occasion into a hall party and are often having aso-ebi. Aso-ebi is a special fabric that is chosen by the celebrant in which all the close family and friends must purchase and sew into a unique outfit with the help of a Nigerian tailor. This has made naming ceremonies, traditionally small and close-knit ceremonies, into larger and bigger parties. Many young Black-British Nigerians welcome this, as it allows more people to celebrate and have large functions within the community. However, this new way of doing naming ceremonies in the UK has come under intense scrutiny by many Yoruba elders, who believe this should remain a closed ceremony with only direct friends and family in attendance and aso-ebi only reserved for the child's immediate family. They believe precious moments like these should only be shared with people known directly to the family, and having large hall parties opens the occasion up to many people – many who have only come for the party and celebrations.

References

David, 'Naming ceremony in Yoruba culture', (Ileoduduwa, 1 February 2017), www.ileoduduwa.com/naming-ceremony-yoruba-culture/#:~:text=The%20most%20common%20are%20from,passing%20of%20a%20family%20elder, accessed 29 June 2021.

David Williams, [online video], 'Yoruba naming ceremony Part 1', (31 January 2017), https://youtu.be/dohzZvp-Dlo, accessed 29 June 2021.

O'Keefe Osborn C., 'What is Kola nut?', (Healthline, 18 September 2018), www.healthline.com/health/kola-nut#:~:text=Kola%20nuts%20have%20a%20bitter,they%20reportedly%20smell%20of%20nutmeg, accessed 29 June 2021.

Soetan L., 'Concept of naming in Yoruba culture', (Ekimogun Descendant, no date), www.ekimogundescendant.org/concept-of-naming-in-yoruba-culture/, accessed 29 June 2021.

The Diet Blogger, 'The choice between bitter Kola or Kola nut?', (Diet 234, no date), https://diet234.com/bitter-kola-kola-nut/, accessed 29 June 2021.

Learning objectives	1. To understand the practices of a Yoruba naming ceremony. 2. To learn at least four Yoruba words. 3. To understand the importance of names in Yoruba culture.
Main activities	1. PowerPoint/pamphlet/tasting foods and analysing items 2. Video 3. Briefly explore the significance of their own names (to be explored in more depth for homework). 4. Complete necessary worksheets.
Homework	1. Questionnaires about their own names should be provided and completed with parents/caregivers to share with the class in the next lesson. 2. The questionnaire should include questions about name meaning, significance, i.e. whether they were named after someone and why etc.

Key Words/New Phrases

Iyo

Oyin

Epo

Orogbo

Eja

Ata

Obi

Destiny names

Acquired names

Panegyrics

Oriki A biku

Olu

In-class lessons:

1. PowerPoint or pamphlet on the Yoruba naming ceremony to be shared with the children. Introduce the Yoruba people at the beginning of the presentation, detailing where they are from, a brief history etc. During the presentation detail the seven items used in the ceremony, explain that they have significant meanings, but do not describe what these are.
2. Next, the children should be given three items of choice from the seven items. Ask them to think about what emotion or feeling they associate with each flavour, and/or which human qualities they associate with the different tastes. After they have shared, resume the presentation and explain what each of the seven items represents.
3. Children should explore and understand how Yoruba ceremonies are taking place in the UK and be able to argue why the recent changes to the ceremony have happened.
4. Share the video listed in the references. Ask the children to think about what they notice about the video. They should then feedback their thoughts to the class.
5. Complete relevant worksheets.

Further guide of future lessons:

1. The importance of names in cultures across the world.

Notes

1 The editors of Encyclopaedia Britannica, '*Yoruba: People*' (Britannica, July 20 1998) <www.britannica.com/topic/Yoruba> accessed 5 July 2021l
2 Ibid.
3 J.T Bendor-Samuel, '*Benue-Congo Languages*' (Britannica, 12, December 2000) <www.britannica.com/topic/Benue-Congo-languages>, accessed 5 July 2021
4 The editors of Encyclopaedia Britannica, '*Yoruba: People*' (Britannica, July 20 1998) <www.britannica.com/topic/Yoruba> accessed 5 July 2021
5 Ibid.
6 L. Soetan '*Concept of naming in Yoruba culture*' (Ekimogun Descendant, no date) <www.ekimogundescendant.org/concept-of-naming-in-yoruba-culture/>, accessed 29 June 2021

10 Local histories – Raphael Albert

Lesson Title: Raphael Albert

Lesson Aims:

1. To learn about Raphael Albert's life
2. To learn about the importance of events he organised in the social context

To learn the following skills:

1. Chronological understanding
2. Knowledge of people
3. Interpretation

National syllabus links

History: To know and understand the history of the British islands as a coherent, chronological narrative, from the earliest times to the present day: how people's lives have shaped this nation and how Britain has influenced and been influenced by the wider world. Understand historical concepts such as continuity and change, cause and consequence, similarity, difference and significance; use them to make connections, draw contrasts, analyse trends and frame historically valid questions; and create their own structured accounts, including written narratives and analyses. Gain historical perspective by placing their growing knowledge into different contexts, understanding the connections between local, regional, national and international history; between cultural, economic, military, political, religious and social history; and between short- and long-term timescales.

Worksheet Colour Code: Green: 7–8 Blue: 8–9 Orange: 9–11

Further outcomes for children:

1. Children will acquire an interest for those who lived in the past and understand the impact they have had on the present.
2. Children will be enabled to learn about significant moments in Black British history.

Teacher resource guide

Who was Raphael Albert?

Raphael was an artist, photographer and promoter born in Grenada, West Indies. He was a twin and the youngest of ten brothers and sisters.[1] Life was difficult for Albert, and he struggled whilst

DOI: 10.4324/9781003194378-11

there to make a living. Often, he'd sell his artwork to tourists on the beach and undertake menial jobs, such as sweeping the floor of a photography studio.[2]

In 1953 he moved to England like many other Caribbean people did at the time.[3] At the time of his travels, Albert was in possession of one suitcase which contained all of his belongings, including an old Kodak camera.[4]

Raphael Albert in London

During the 1950s, when an influx of West Indians travelled to Britain during the Windrush period, it was common for men to take a job at London Transport or the post office. Instead, Raphael attended college, in Ealing (Thames Valley College[5]). There he studied photography, whilst simultaneously working a job at Lyons cake factory.[6] Once he graduated, he established himself as a freelance photographer.

Life as a photographer and promoter

Albert's freelance career began with photographing local dance promoters. He later became the official photographer of the Miss Jamaica pageant for the *West Indian World* newspaper. He would also photograph for prominent British West Indian newspapers: *Gleaner*, *Caribbean Times* and *New World*.[7] Whilst Albert's career seemed to be taking off, he became a father in 1963. He was thus forced to look for a second career to make enough money to support his family.[8]

During the 1970s, in response to catering directly to the Black gaze and specifically creating and fostering Black cultural spaces, he was led to create and launch the Miss Black and Beautiful contest,[9] before going on to create Miss West Indies in Great Britain.[10] At the time, there was nothing like it. The popularity of the pageant grew and Albert went on to promote Miss Grenada (UK), Miss Teenager of the West Indies in Great Britain, Model of the Year and Miss Black and Beautiful.[11] Albert ran these pageants from his own company, called 'Albert promotions'.[12] He understood the importance of documenting the cultural life of West Indians during early settlement in the UK and wanted his photographs to be seen on this basis. For many years, Albert continued to be a "formidable presence as a promoter and photographer".[13] The pageants ran for 30 years, and Albert also created a magazine during this time, called *Charisma*, in 1984.[14]

Raphael Albert's legacy

Albert's pageants challenged conventional ideas of beauty. The idea of beauty was defined by white characteristics in the cultural, social and political context of the time.[15] The pageants were more than beauty contests – they provided a space for African-Caribbeans to construct their own identities under a set of standards from a decolonial point of view that placed Black people at the centre.

References

Autograph, 'About the artist', (Autograph, no date), https://autograph.org.uk/exhibitions/miss-black-and-beautiful, accessed 5 July 2021.

Henry J., 'Raphael albert obituary', (The Guardian, 18 December 2009), www.theguardian.com/theguardian/2009/dec/18/raphael-albert-obituary, accessed 5, July 2021.

Smyth D., 'Black and beautiful in Raphael Albert's vintage photographs of beauty contests', (1854, 13 June 2008), www.1854.photography/2018/06/black-beautiful-albert/, accessed 5 July 2021.

Learning objectives	1. Learn about the significance of Black beauty pageants in 60s–70s Britain. 2. Learn about the life of Raphael Albert.
Main activities	1. PowerPoint/pamphlet 2. Talent pageant/alternative task: photography 3. Worksheets
Homework	1. Poster/banner for talent pageant.

In-class lessons:

1. Show the children a PowerPoint or give them an informative handout on Raphael Albert and his endeavours – emphasise the context of the beauty pageant and his creativity. Explain that pageants were focused on instilling cultural pride and creating spaces where the Black community could come together and celebrate themselves. Expand on the importance of Black pride in the context of white supremacy and that these cultural spaces were being created at a time where Black people were pushing back against racist narratives that deemed them not to be considered beautiful. Organising pageants was also a form of artistic expression for Albert. Finally, the pageants were important as a way to establish community.

2. Following on from the aforementioned, explain to the children that they will partake in a classroom talent and culture show like Albert's. Allow the children, in two groups, to brainstorm ideas on the organisation of the cultural show (how they would like it to go) and then feedback these ideas to the teacher. Collectively the class will decide how it should be organised based on everyone's ideas. The cultural show should take place in another lesson or in assembly where possible.

   Alternative task: Children in groups of four should be given a throwaway (disposable) camera. They should then take pictures of things that represent Black British culture i.e. in the class or in the playground. Once the pictures are developed, a small exhibition in the classroom should be developed.

3. Relevant worksheets.

Key Words/New Phrases

Pageant

Cultural life

Promoter

Miss Black and Beautiful

The plenary

Events and promoters are incredibly important in Black British culture, specifically because there was no safe space to 'be' following the years after their migration. Raphael Albert's organisation of events left an impact and created a space for Black people to self-define.

Further guide of future lessons:

1. The importance of cultural events in the Black British community.
2. Notable Black British event promoters.

BLAM

Name _____   **Year** _____

BRISTOL BUS BOYCOTT

What is discrimination?

_____

_____

_____

Which American civil rights leaders inspired Paul Stevenson to start the boycott?

_____

_____

_____

_____

_____

_____

_____

_____

Figure 11.2 Worksheet for ages 8–9

Name _____ **Year** _____

BRISTOL BUS BOYCOTT

Fill in the blanks

In 1963, ____ _____ arranged a job interview for ___ _____ to join the Bristol Omnibus Company as a conductor. At the time, the company didn't know that Bailey was a Black West Indian man. When he turned up for the interview, he was turned away because of the colour of his skin.

Racist discrimination in employment, housing, or education was known as the _____ ___. Black people in Britain also faced violent attacks by gangs of young white men called _____ ____.

On 30th April 1963 the ____ _____ community launched a _____ against the bus company in response to its racist policy. The boycott lasted four months. The campaign helped bring about Britain's first laws against racial _____.

teddy boys   **Paul Stevenson**

colour bar   **West Indian**   **boycott**

discrimination   **Guy Bailey**

Figure 11.2 (Continued)

BLAM

Name _____ **Year** _____

BRISTOL BUS BOYCOTT

Draw a mural of the leaders of the Bristol Bus Boycott

Figure 11.2 (Continued)

Name
_____

Year
_____

BRISTOL BUS BOYCOTT

What year did the Bristol Bus Boycott and Martin Luther King Jr's 'I have a dream' speech take place?

_____

What did the two Race Relations Acts of 1965 and 1968 cover?

_____
_____
_____
_____
_____
_____
_____
_____

Figure 11.3 Worksheet for ages 9–11

Name _____

Year _____

BRISTOL BUS BOYCOTT

Match names to the right statement

A. Rosa Parks   D. Paul Stevenson
B. Roy Hackett   E. Harold Wilson
C. Guy Bailey   F. Raghbir Singh

1. Arranged a job interview for Guy Bailey to join the Bristol Omnibus Company as a bus conductor. Hosted a press conference announcing the boycott to the media. _____

2. Was turned away for a job interview at the Bristol Omnibus Company. _____

3. A Jamaican organiser of the Bristol Bus Boycott who was later involved in organising St. Paul's Carnival. _____

4. Afro-American woman who refused to give up her seat for a white passenger, kicking off the Montgomery Bus Boycott (1955 - 1956). _____

5. Became Bristol's first non-white bus conductor in September 1963. _____

6. Prime Minister when the Race Relations Acts of 1965 and 1968 were passed. _____

Figure 11.3 (Continued)

Name _____   **Year** _____

BRISTOL BUS BOYCOTT

Write up your opinion about the outcome of the boycott. Why was this victory a success for more than just Black and Asian bus drivers?

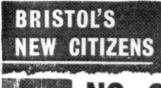

BRISTOL'S NEW CITIZENS

The Full Facts On A Controversial Issue

Why are there no coloured men working on Bristol's buses? If you take a bus ride in London, Oxford, Birmingham or West Bromwich the chances are the the conductor comes from Jamaica or Barbados— you may even find the driver does too. But in Bristol there are no such opportunities for the new citizens. Evening Post reporter Malcolm Smith tells you why in in this full inquiry.

NO COLOUR BAR ON OUR BUSES

The coloured bus conductor is a cheerful and willing character you will find collecting fares in many a British city. But not in Bristol. He is a fellow most anv

—but no jobs either for the immigrants

EVENING POST

_____

_____

_____

_____

_____

_____

_____

_____

_____

Figure 11.3 (Continued)

Notes

1 Madge Dresser, Black and White on the Buses: The 1963 Colour Bar Dispute, www.victo-riacountyhistory.ac.uk/explore/sites/explore/files/explore_assets/2010/03/22/bri_ide_Band-WOnTheBuses6.pdf

2 Elizabeth Jones, 'The Bristol bus boycott of 1963', (Black History Month, 7 October 2018), www.blackhistorymonth.org.uk/article/section/bhm-heroes/the-bristol-bus-boycott-of-1963/

3 Madge Dresser, 'The Bristol bus boycott: A watershed moment for Black Britain', (Bristol Museums), www.bristolmuseums.org.uk/stories/bristol-bus-boycott/

4 Claire Mansour, 'The Cross-national diffusion of the American civil rights movement: the example of the Bristol bus boycott of 1963', *Images on the Move* (2014), https://journals.openedition.org/miranda/6360

5 Madge Dresser, Black and White on the Buses: The 1963 Colour Bar Dispute, www.victo-riacountyhistory.ac.uk/explore/sites/explore/files/explore_assets/2010/03/22/bri_ide_Band-WOnTheBuses6.pdf

6 Virgillo Hunter, 'The Bristol bus boycott of 1963', (Black Past, 9 June 2019), www.black-past.org/global-african-history/the-bristol-bus-boycott-of-1963/; Fiona Raleigh, 'What happened during the Bristol bus boycott?', (Kaplan), www.kaplanpathways.com/about/news/what-happened-during-the-bristol-bus-boycott/

12 Black British resistance groups

Lesson Title: Black resistance groups in the UK from the 60s to the 80s

Lesson Aims:

1. To be able to identify the main Black resistance groups in the UK
2. To understand social history and how it relates to formation of identity
3. To be able to identify change over a period of time

To learn the following skills:

1. To recognise the effect of the past on the future
2. To learn and apply new historical and legal terms

Links to the national syllabus

History:

- To understand how British people have been influenced by others all over the world
- To be able to produce well-constructed selection and organisation of historical facts, dates and general information
- To establish clear narratives within the time period
- To understand the complexity of historical events and that they are part of a long arc of development and change
- To grasp the concept of different contexts and how local events can impact a period

Art:

- To create meaningful art that records personal observation (in this case of society)

Further outcomes for children:

- Develop chronologically organised thinking skills
- Be able to verbalise and debate about their thoughts and feelings on topics
- Be able to link the past and present through events

The plenary

How did the British Black Power movement come about?

During the latter part of the 20th century, British race relation tension was at an all-time high. This was due to an amalgamation of harassment from police, lack of educational, employment or housing opportunities and legal discrimination in the courts that led Black people to reject normative white

DOI: 10.4324/9781003194378-13

supremacy and take more drastic actions for the circumstances they were facing. Black resistance groups began flexing their muscles in the late 1960s, which seemed to be sparked by Stokely Carmichael's speech at the Roundhouse, London, in 1967, at which many prominent Black rights activists were present. It also prompted police harassment/agitation around this. Within the week, the UCPA (a civil rights organisation for Black and Asian migrants) expelled all of its white members and the Trinidadian revolutionary Michael X was arrested on charges of inciting racial violence, and within the year, the Black Panthers were founded. It seemed as though Carmichael's speech was the driving force and trigger for Black people in Britain to take their destiny into their own hands.[1]

British Black Panthers

The British Black Panthers (BBP) were founded in 1968 by a Nigerian playwright named Obi Egbuna in London's renowned Notting Hill. This was until he was arrested on false charges of threatening police, which is when Trinidadian physician Altheia Jones-Lecointe and one of the Mangrove Nine took his place in leadership. The Black Panthers in Britain took their name, aesthetics and values from the Black Panthers in America, rocking leather jackets and berets and using a raised fist as a sign of solidarity for their brothers and sisters across the pond.[2] However, there was a fundamental difference in the practical element of resistance, such as legal strategy, which set the British Panthers apart: the claim that Black British vernacular could not be understood by police when interacting with Black people, hence why misunderstandings and violence took place. They were pioneers in reflecting the Black British experience in courts.[3] The Panthers were fundamental in drumming up support from white sympathisers during the 'Mangrove Nine' case, including political groups and trade unionists who wanted to support the nine. This was due to their rejection of narrow identity politics in exchange for more of a class-based view on racism under new leader Altheia Jones-Lecointe. It was, then, an inevitable move for Darcus Howe to join the British Black Panther Party due to being on trial with its centre force. Howe advocated for Black and white collaboration, particularly the white working class, as he viewed them as a fluid group who soaked up immigrants from around the globe, as opposed to the white elites who viewed them as ignorant and lazy.[4] Darcus Howe joined the Black Panthers swiftly after the Mangrove Nine case. Shortly afterwards, there was a new publication from them, called *Freedom News*, which disassociated the group from its previous Leninist rhetoric and encouraged the community to speak up about racism in their everyday lives.[5] The Panthers under the leadership of Altheia Jones-Lecointe had a different dynamic; she made Black women who were fighting for racial equality more visible and fought for the sexual rights of Black women – anyone with sexist views in the BBP didn't last long. Although she was not officially made leader, under her direction, the BBP membership increased by more than 3000 people and she created many community outreach programs, similar to the ones in America made by resistance groups there.[6]

Race Today Collective

The *Race Today Collective* was a bi-monthly magazine and political group that focused on the advancement of Black people in Britain and how oppression in legal, medical, employment, education and housing intrinsically affected Black Britons. They also focused on how to put a stop to police brutality, and through their intersectional, radical nature were able to link Black struggles to other class and gender fights. The magazine did not always take such a radical approach. Under Peter Watson's editorship, it took a more conservative rhetoric; however, ideological differences sparked an internal upheaval in 1972, splitting from the International Race Relations Council it originated from in 1958. With their freer editorial reign, Darcus Howe became chief editor, which led to more of a focus on the everyday strife of Black people alongside rejection of ethnic nationalism (similar to *Freedom News*) and also looked into the explosion of artistic Black expression that had taken place in the metropolitan areas of the UK; *Race Today Collective* wanted to prevent London-centric narratives. In fact, *Race Today Collective* consistently pioneered themselves as an organ for global revolutionary action, which was helped along by their campaign to "Free the Third World". Possibly most importantly, the *Race Today Collective* magazine rejected the notion white elites placed on Black people – that they were helpless and victims – spinning it on its head by encouraging Black people to be self-sufficient within their communities and, essentially, have the power to carve out their own destinies. *Race Today Collective* was instrumental in aiding the Brixton riots, through setting up the Brixton Defence Committee to campaign for amnesty for those arrested in the riots, to having enough influence within the community to be entrusted by leaders of the riots to discuss how to move forward. Members of the *Race Today Collective* include Leila Hassan Farrukh Dhondy, Gus John, Linton Kwesi Johnson and Darcus Howe. Both the *Race Today Collective* magazine and group were discontinued in 1988.[7]

The Fasimbas

The Fasimbas were a dynamic organization that emerged in response to the pressing need for cultural and educational empowerment within the Black British community, particularly among the descendants of colonial migrants from the Caribbean. Comprising the "young, gifted, and black," the Fasimbas were a collective of individuals who were either British-educated or British-born and were deeply committed to rectifying the misinformation and omissions in the British educational curriculum that affected Black youths. The group would provide supplementary education on Saturdays, education in African and Caribbean history, political education, martial arts classes, bookstalls, public meetings, plays, dances and electronics. The Sound System Jah Shaka was inspired by the Fasimbas.[8]

Their roots can be traced back to the South East London Parent's Organization (SELPO), an initiative created to address the systemic problems in education that marginalized and neglected Black students. The Fasimbas initially began as an informal youth branch of SELPO, where their focus was to combat the prevailing racial biases and educational deficits in the curriculum.

As the group's influence and membership grew, it naturally evolved into the Youth and Political Wing of SELPO, reflecting their increasing involvement in addressing broader socio-political issues that affected the Black community. By 1971, they officially adopted the name "The Fasimbas," solidifying their identity as a distinct and influential force within the Black British community. The Fasimbas played a vital role in raising awareness, promoting education, and advocating for the rights and interests of Black British youth, leaving a lasting impact on the struggle for racial equality and social justice in the United Kingdom.

The Black Unity and Freedom Party

The Black Unity and Freedom Party (BUFP) was a small group created by Leila Hassan, Ricky Cambridge and George Joseph that materialised from the fragments of the UCPA in 1970. They propagated themselves as culturally Leninist, with their journal *Black Voice* encouraging white and Black proletariat consensus against capitalism to override racism. They had strictly Black membership and published stories from all over the African diaspora from an anti-consumerist stance. The BUFP were mostly directly involved in organising with other Black resistance groups, for example with the Black Liberation Front, to set up the annual African Liberation Day. They were also involved in giving lectures or organising meetings about Black cultural heritage and aided protest and information campaigns such as Black People's Day of Action and the

'Tottenham three are innocent' campaign. The group disintegrated in 1999 after a couple of members of the party wanted to have a more Afro-centric rhetoric – therefore forming the African People's Liberation Organisation instead.[9]

Case studies

The Mangrove Nine

The Mangrove restaurant was the heart of the Black community in London, which served as a safe space where Black intellectuals could discuss ideas about how to move forward with resistance against the government and police.

This is how it was described by the *International Times* in 1969, a publication that was associated with sharing stories outside of the norm.

> The Mangrove Restaurant, All Saints Rd., W11. Is the central eating place for the black community In Notting Hill. It is the one clean, late night social centre which also serves good food, and black families use it as a meeting place as well as a place of entertainment.

It was also a melting pot of classes where Black people of different backgrounds merged ideas together and eventually formed a coalition to fight the police campaign against the Mangrove.

The Mangrove was continuously raided on multiple occasions from 1969 to 1970 on the grounds of drug possession and serving food without a licence. However, no drugs were ever found and the licence in question was discriminatorily removed from Frank Crichlow, the owner of the Mangrove. Darcus Howe, being inspired by Black Power in his native country Trinidad and also his travels to Brooklyn where he joined the Student Nonviolent Coordinating Committee (SNCC), advised Chrichlow to take to the streets and demonstrate with the Black community. Chrichlow agreed despite possible closure of his restaurant, and the demonstration preparations began.

The demonstration took place on the 9th of August 1970 and they planned to protest outside of three police stations. By the time they got to Notting Hill, there was an extremely overbearing police presence, with documents showing that 588 constables, 84 sergeants, 29 inspectors and four chief inspectors were available that day – in sum there were 705 police officers present at the time. The march consisted of about 150 people. The press's reaction was paramount in stirring up confusion and disdain towards the march by the British public as neither broadsheets nor tabloids had conceptualised the real motives behind it. Instead, they focused on the details of police injury or used it as an opportunity to thrust political narratives forward. For example, the *Telegraph* in 1970 stated that the march made an immigration bill proposing severe cuts to immigration justifiable. Nine people were arrested and charged with various crimes, one being incitement of riot.

The magistrate subjected the prosecution to serious scrutiny, shot down their main arguments against the defendants and concluded that the violence and riot was spontaneous and not pre-planned. The charges of riot were dropped, and the demonstrators were sent for sentence at the Old Bailey for the charges of affray and possession of an offensive weapon. However, the director of public prosecutions reintroduced the charge of riot before the sentencing hearing, an action that could be done without rhyme or reason in the courts at the time. The 'Mangrove Nine', consisting of Darcus Howe, Frank Crichlow, Rhodan Gordan, Altheia Jones-Lecointe, Barbara Beese, Godfrey Miller, Rupert Glasgow Boyce, Anthony Carlisle Innis and Rothwell Kentish were now facing a possibility of ten years in jail.

Support for the movement flooded in both domestically and internationally, with many Black Power grassroots organisations carrying out community organising such as handing out leaflets

Name _____ Class _____

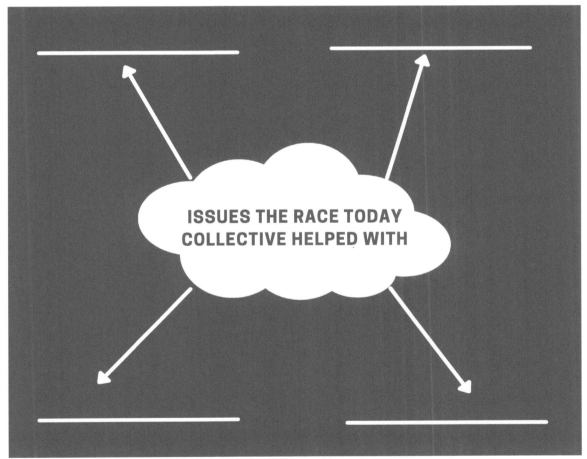

Figure 12.4 Worksheet for ages 7–8

Name _____   Class _____

RACE TODAY COLLECTIVE

The Race Today magazine office was based in Brixton. If you had your own political magazine, where would you base it? Draw your office in the place you chose below. You can choose anywhere in the world!

Figure 12.5 Worksheet for ages 8–9

Name _____   Class _____

RACE TODAY COLLECTIVE

PLEASE COMPLETE THE CROSSWORD PUZZLE BELOW

Across

6. Ordinary people being seen as the main body of an organisation

8. Use of excessive force by law enforcement

Down

1. Where people live- there were many issues surrounding black people gaining access to this

2. Needing no outside help to satisfy basic needs

3. Nick name given to poorer parts of the world. The Race Today Collective had a campaign to free it .

4. Focusing solely on London

5. A protest that took place in a well known part of South London in 1981

7. Editor of Race Today Collective magazine

BLAM

Figure 12.6 Worksheet for ages 9–11

A DREAM OF ENGLAND

Draw what you think the author is "dreaming" of in the poem, when they imagine England

Provided by Black Learning Achievement and Mental Health CIC

Figure 13.1 Worksheet for ages 7–8

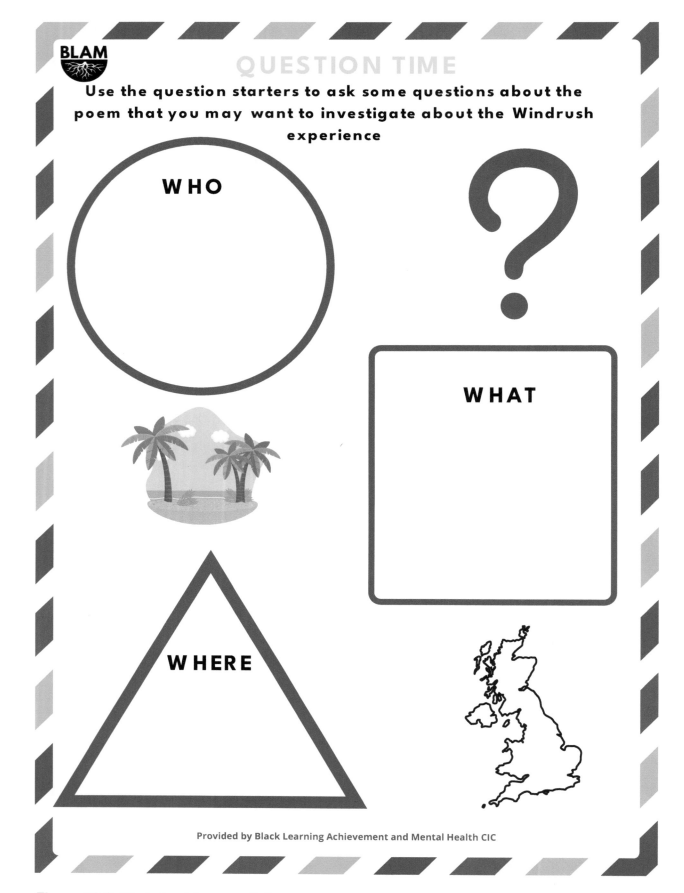

QUESTION TIME

Use the question starters to ask some questions about the poem that you may want to investigate about the Windrush experience

WHO

?

WHAT

WHERE

Provided by Black Learning Achievement and Mental Health CIC

Figure 13.2 Worksheet for ages 8–9

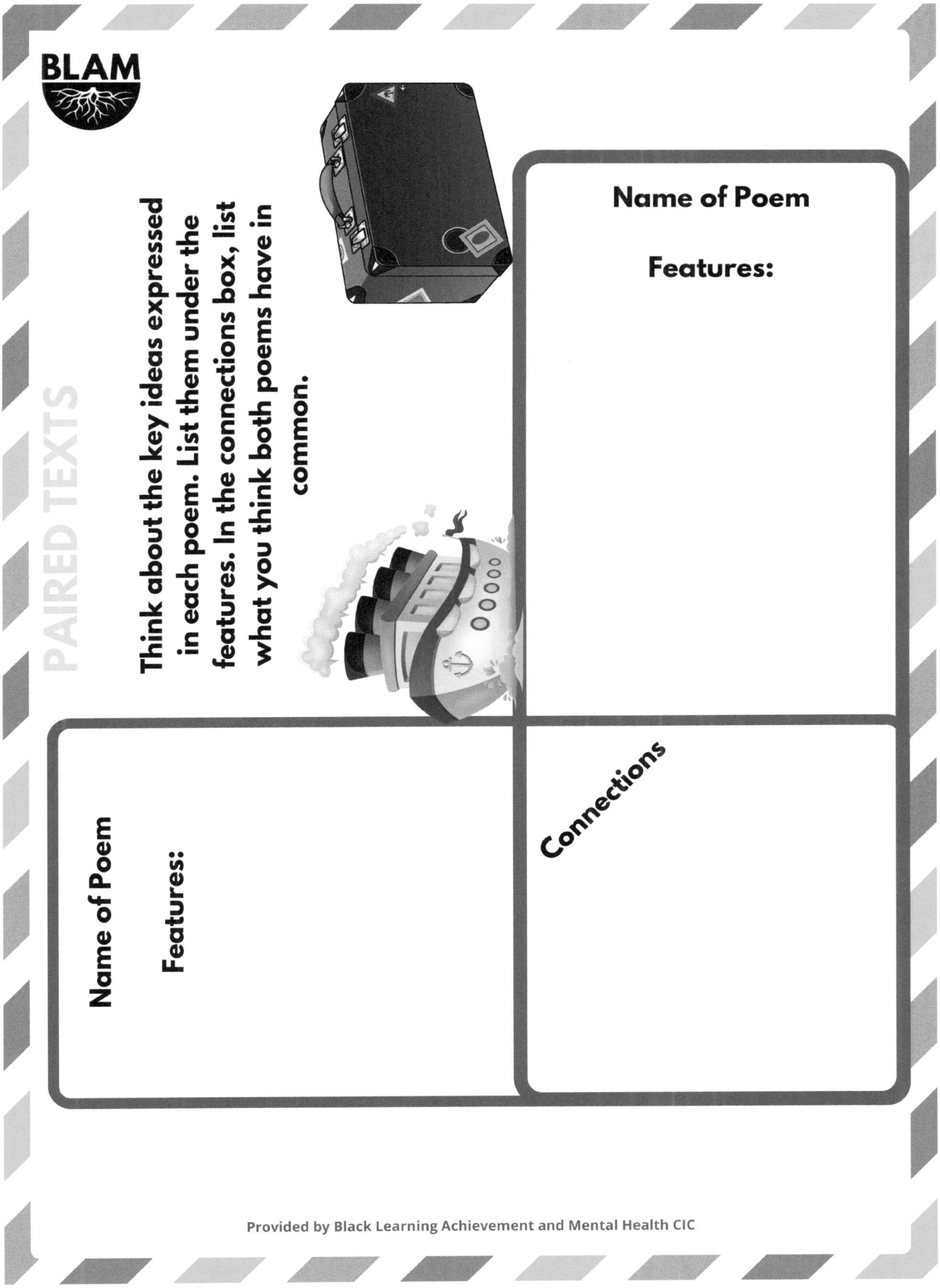

BLAM

PAIRED TEXTS

Think about the key ideas expressed in each poem. List them under the features. In the connections box, list what you think both poems have in common.

Name of Poem

Features:

Name of Poem

Features:

Connections

Figure 13.3 Worksheet for ages 9–11

Notes

1 Museum of London, 'How did the Empire Windrush Change London?', (Museum of London, 2020), https://www.museumoflondon.org.uk/discover/how-did-empire-windrush-change-london-docklands, accessed 03 August 2023.

2 Lowe H., 'An introduction to Andrea Levy's *Small Island*' [online], (The British Library, 4 October 2018), www.bl.uk/windrush/articles/an-introduction-to-andrea-levys-small-island, accessed 24 May 2022.

3 Berry J., I Dream of Leavin, *Poems on the Underground*, TFL [online], https://poemsontheunderground.org/a-dream-of-leavin, accessed 24 May 2022.

4 Breeze J., Dreamer, *Poems on the Underground*, TFL [online], https://poemsontheunderground.org/dreamer, accessed 24 May 2022.

5 Nichols G., Epilogue, *Poems on the Underground*, TFL [online], https://poemsontheunderground.org/epilogue, accessed, 24 May 2022.

6 BBC Studios, Hortense Dreams of England [online video], 14 January 2013, www.youtube.com/watch?v=u_s1dhQ5Pzo, accessed 24 May 2022.

14 Dub

The skeleton of Reggae music

Lesson Aims:

To develop an aural memory and understanding of dub music composition.

1.

a. To listen and respond to dub music samples from the 1970s
b. To identify the characteristics of dub music
c. To make meaningful links between the sociocultural norms of the Jamaican-British community in the 1970s and compositional styles of dub music
d. To improvise some ideas for 'toasting' to a dub music sample

2. To learn the following skills:

● Listening
● Sharing ideas
● Connection finding
● Innovation
● Improvisation
● Composition (music)
● Creative expression

Subject areas: Music (inc. music history), Science

Pupils will use music samples to analyse and build an auditory memory of dub music. They will learn about how the compositional styles of dub music originate from Afro-Caribbean rhythms in Reggae music. They will use speaking and listening activities to engage in meaningful dialogue about the similarities and differences between dub music and some other genres that they are already familiar with. Pupils will use their improvisational skills to compose 'toasting' lyrics and melodies to a dub music sample backing of their choice. Their understanding of compositional ideas in dub music should also highlight dub music as a major cultural revolution in electronic music genres and amplify the skillset of the musicians as scientists, given that the main recording processes of dub are reliant on sound engineering skills and celebrate an intersection of creative expression and scientific inquiry. Ultimately, the teaching and learning of music in this unit must be framed through the application of prior knowledge and understanding about sound in Key Stage 2 Science, including vibrations and soundwaves.

DOI: 10.4324/9781003194378-15

National syllabus links

Taken from the National Curriculum Framework Document

Music:

Key Stage 2 pupils should appreciate and understand a wide range of high-quality live and recorded music drawn from different traditions and from great composers and musicians – develop an understanding of the history of music.

Science:

Sound

Pupils should be taught to:

- identify how sounds are made, associating some of them with something vibrating
- recognise that vibrations from sounds travel through a medium to the ear
- find patterns between the pitch of a sound and features of the object that produced it
- find patterns between the volume of a sound and the strength of the vibrations that produced it – recognise that sounds get fainter as the distance from the sound source increases.

The plenary: background information

Dub music origins

Dub music originated in Kingston, Jamaica, and was 'rehomed' (Walker, 2020)[1] in London, England, due to the migration of the Windrush community in the UK. Dub music is often considered to be a sensation and an experience that channels the concept and fantasy of Afrofuturism – a transcending, liberating and fictional reality of the African diaspora. The 'vibrations' of dub are created by layering different Bass rhythms and creating an echo that sets the mood and energy of what is considered to be the skeleton of Reggae music.

The word 'dub' has a pluralised meaning in the music industry. In a sound engineering context, it refers to the act of *doubling* an audio, which is essentially what has inspired the name of this culturally layered music genre.

www.theguardian.com/music/2020/sep/27/soundtrack-of-a-city-how-dub-reggae-shook-and-shaped-london

Characteristics of dub music

VERSIONS/DOUBLES IN DUB MUSIC

Versions or doubles in dub music is a technology used in the recording process by the sound engineers and recording artists. The purpose is to emphasise the Bass of the guitar, which later acts as a reference for the DJ to 'toast' (rap) to. At times, the version/double is used to develop a soundscape in dub music and can feature birds singing or water flowing, which creates a multi-sensory experience for the listener.

Toasting, or chatting, in dub music is the act of rapping or speaking rhythmically over dub music. The names of the recording artist who 'toasts' to a record is often varied. In many cases, they are called the DeeJay, and toasting is also considered a style of deejaying.

Teacher resource guide

1. Mad Professor – Dub Me Crazy 3: The African Connection/Full[2]
Mad Professor (b.1955) is one of the leading Black British pioneers of dub music. Born in Guyana as Fraser, his love for electronics and music technology engrossed him into a world of innovation, cultivated and self-preserved in his South London home.

He is best known for his Dub Me Crazy collection, which explores the African influence in dub music and culture.

Key words and phrases

Dub – Dub is a music genre which is considered a subgenre of Reggae. It was electronically produced by musicians in the Caribbean diaspora during the 1960s and 1970s in cities like Kingston, Jamaica, and London, England.

Genre (music) – A genre is a type or category of an art form. Dub music is a genre in its own right, but is also loosely connected to Reggae as a subgenre (a genre that grew out of another). It is also credited as a genre which influenced other genres such as punk and Hip-Hop.

Toast – To rap, or talk rhythmically over a dub music sample.

In-class lessons

Before the lesson, teachers need to have a video or audio recording of Mad Professor – Dub Me Crazy 3: The African Connection/Full for the pupils to listen and respond to.

Lesson objective: to respond to the compositional characteristics of dub music

Differentiation guide: *The activities will be differentiated by outcome. The listening and speaking part of today's lesson should encourage meaningful discussion around the classification of the compositional features in dub music.*

Expressive response (two parts)

Play 'The African Connection' by Mad Professor. It is the first track of Dub Me Crazy 3.

On the first listen, encourage pupils to close their eyes and put their heads down to imagine the mood of the piece. Their bodies should be still – they could be sitting or standing idly.

On the second listen, encourage pupils to walk slowly around the classroom, using their bodies to represent the physical interactions that they think could be happening to this piece of music. To guide their 'expressive response', ask them to imagine that this piece of music belonged to a movie or a story. *What could be happening?*

The call for reparations is often identified as a debate or an ongoing case, given that up until present day, the United Kingdom has never formally apologised for its colonial crimes. It is also sometimes argued that slavery happened such a long time ago, that we ought to forget about it.

However, the socioeconomic disadvantages of the intersections of slavery, colonialism and imperialism continue to vary and persist harm onto its descendants – including exploitative labour, mental and intellectual trauma, coercion into war, poverty, illiteracy, little healthcare access and the harsh effects of climate change.

Teacher resource guide

Afua Hirsch's article 'The case for British slavery reparations can no longer be brushed aside', https://www.theguardian.com/commentisfree/2020/jul/09/british-slavery-reparations-economy-compensation

Use Afua Hirsch's article to support the children's understanding of how to use articles as a reliable source for information.

Key words and phrases

Reparations – A payment given back to a community to make amends for wrongdoing.
Owed – An obligation to pay or repay something back to the person or group of people you took it from.

Before this lesson, pupils will have refreshed their knowledge and understanding of the transatlantic slave trade and how it has harmed Afro-Caribbean communities for centuries thereafter. This lesson will frame some planning ideas that can be developed into a digital literacy campaign in weeks to come.

In-class lessons

Lesson objective: To plan a digital literacy campaign for the reparations movement.
Differentiation guide: *The activities will be differentiated by outcome. The listening and speaking part of today's lesson should encourage innovative ideas and solutions among a dynamic group of learners.*

Observations

Begin by sharing several examples of historical political campaigns with the pupils. You can project them to the whole class using an interactive whiteboard or print copies of them to hand. Some examples of these may include the Black Panther Party mantra posters, Barack Obama's 'Hope' poster by Shepard Fairey, the 1943 "We can do it' poster by J. Howard Miller, etc. Use the guiding questions to aid the pupils' collective observation skills.

Guiding questions

● What do you see?
● Which of these posters do you recognise?
● How might these posters have been useful?
● If you could come up with a name for these types of posters, what would it be?

- How are these posters similar and how are they different?
- These posters were used for political campaigns. What do you think is meant by this term?
- We don't use posters as much as we did in the past. What are some newer ways of spreading information?
- If you had to pick a cause, what would you make a campaign about?
- If you had to make a checklist for what makes a good campaign poster, what would you include?

Note-taking

Show pupils the video of Trevor Noah explaining the reparations argument in the context of the United States: 'The Reparations Debate: Should America Compensate the Descendants of Slaves?' | *The Daily Show*.[1]

Play it again. This time, ask pupils to take notes, or brainstorm around the word 'Reparations' – what do they now understand by this word? Have they heard this word before? Ask children to pair-share a community/ethnic group that they think might be owed reparations by the United Kingdom. (They may either suggest a number of examples or become overwhelmed by the complexity of this question. In the latter case, move onto the next step.)

Introduction and inquiry

Read Afua Hirsch's article to pupils ('The case for British slavery reparations can no longer be brushed aside', https://www.theguardian.com/commentisfree/2020/jul/09/british-slavery-reparations-economy-compensation), and ask them to give you ideas about interesting or meaningful words that need to be underlined. Alternatively, they can read the article and underline their chosen vocabulary terms as a group. Can they add their newfound words to their notes or use them in their worksheet guide to plan their poster campaign for reparations?

Closing reflection

Closing question for Years 3 and 4: What would be the best way to develop our worksheets into information online? How would we create and send the information? Which app could we use?

Closing idea for Year 5: Play pupils 'We Built This' – Musical Performance from *black-ish* Season 4 Premiere and ask pupils to discuss how this video makes the viewer informed about slavery and what the descendants of transatlantic slavery are 'owed'. (You could also unpack what it means to be owed something, if your class has a mild vocabulary range.)

Closing question for Years 5 and 6: The case for reparations is often called a 'debate'. Why do you think this is?

Worksheet Colour Code: Green: 7–8 Blue: 8–9 Orange: 9–11

Year 4 activity suggestion

Pupils can design a poster, in a similar style to the resources used in the observations starter.

Year 5 activity suggestion

Pupils can create a 'movie reel' to develop their dialogue ideas for what they will say in their campaign.

POSTER TEMPLATE

Design a poster for the Reparations movement. Use today's examples to help you.

Provided by Black Learning Achievement and Mental Health CIC

Figure 15.1 Worksheet for ages 7–8

'Punch in the Face' – JME

⁴ *Play 'Punch in the Face' by JME. On the first listen, ask the pupils to close their eyes and listen carefully to the language. On the second listen, ask pupils to jot down three words that they have heard in the song that they would use with their friends that they might not use with their teacher.*

Guiding questions

- What was the song about?
- Why do you think the song was written?
- If you had to direct the music video to this song, what would it look like?
- Where in the world has this song been created? Explain your answer.
- Who might listen to a song like this, and why?
- How old/new do you think this song is, and why?
- Do you think everyone can relate to or understand this song? Explain your answer.
- Which words did you jot down?
- Why might you choose to use these words with your friends, and not your teacher?

Storytelling and translation

Announce to children that the song they have listened to is written and performed in Black British English, and if they listen to music genres that use similar words and phrases, then they have heard this language before. If they use some of the vocabulary that they have heard and spoken about in their own speech and language, then they are fluent in BBE. Affirm audiences that are proficient in BBE by telling them not to be ashamed of BBE, and that the ability to speak and understand it is a language skill. BBE words that they may speak with their friends and not with their teacher is because they may feel that they need to protect the language and its identity among Black British speakers – which is understandable.

For audiences that are new to BBE

Hand out printed copies of the lyrics to 'Punch in the Face' and ask children to get their highlighters ready. In pairs, they should highlight unfamiliar words in the song and discuss what they think the meanings are. *Why did the artist choose to use Black British English to tell us this story?*

For audiences that are proficient in BBE

Hand out printed copies of the lyrics to 'Punch in the Face' and ask children to get their highlighters ready. In pairs, they should highlight what they consider to be the most important phrases in the song. *How do they help us understand the message that the artist wanted to share with us?*

Divide children into groups of three, with one narrator and two actors. The narrator will read aloud the verses from 'Punch in the Face' and the two actors will act out the events that correspond with the language. If there is time, perform some group sequences to the class, to begin framing the worksheet activities.

Closing

Begin the worksheets, and start drafting any questions to send off to JME as a class. Encourage the pupils to ask him about the song and the Black British English terms that sound unfamiliar

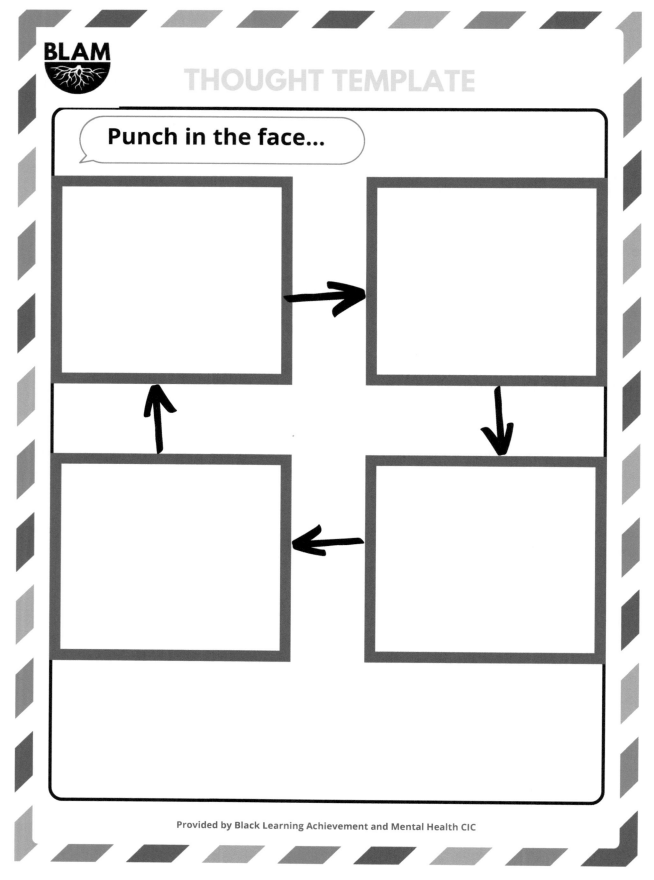

Figure 16.1 Worksheet for ages 7–8

Figure 16.2 Worksheet for ages 8–9

17 Imagery and imperialism

The royal family, empire and colonialism

Lesson Aims:

To make links between the British monarchy and lived experiences of colonialism within historical and modern-day empire.

1.

a. To understand the concept of empire
b. To identify colonialism as a system of harm
c. To consider the long-term effects of colonialism
d. To analyse the implications of the royal family in the lived experiences of today's world

2. To learn the following skills:

● Comparing and contrasting
● Speaking, listening and sharing of ideas
● Critical thinking
● Research
● Analysis of sources
● Opinion forming
● Debate

Subject areas: History, Literacy

*Teachers will facilitate this program of study by using British propaganda as a focal point of discussion, debate and exploration. The debate statement to be explored will be "**The royal family is outdated**". Over time, pupils will use their learning journey to consider whether they are for or against this statement. Pupils will use planning formas to begin collating ideas for their response to the statement and analysis of British propaganda. To deepen critical understanding, teachers should guide children to investigate the symbolism used in British propaganda and the role that this has played in establishing and sustaining the interests of the British Empire. To embark on a clear and defined opinion about the British Empire and its global impact, pupils will need to partake in research. Pupils will use their historical inquiry skills such as the identification and comparison of primary and secondary sources in order to begin developing an informed opinion of the British monarchy. Pupils will engage in a planned debate to express their opinions in reference to the knowledge that they have acquired. Please note that research can be participatory, given that pupils represent a student demographic of children who belong to ethnic groups that have been impacted negatively by colonialism. For example, British*

DOI: 10.4324/9781003194378-18

Igbo-Nigerian pupils may have relatives who experienced elements of the Biafran War, and British Jamaican pupils may know elders who were encouraged to board Empire Windrush *in search of the 'mother country' and so on.*

National syllabus links

Taken from the National Curriculum Framework Document

English:

Explain and discuss their understanding of what they have read, including through formal presentations and debates, maintaining a focus on the topic and using notes where necessary provide reasoned justifications for their views.

History:

Key Stage 2 pupils should continue to develop a chronologically secure knowledge and understanding of British, local and world history, establishing clear narratives within and across the periods they study. They should note connections, contrasts and trends over time and develop the appropriate use of historical terms. They should regularly address and sometimes devise historically valid questions about change, cause, similarity and difference, and significance. They should construct informed responses that involve thoughtful selection and organisation of relevant historical information. They should understand how our knowledge of the past is constructed from a range of sources.

The plenary: background information

The British Empire

The British Empire began in the late 1500s under the rule of Queen Elizabeth I and reigned over 400 million people, making it the largest empire in history. It was a genocidal system which involved the invasion of multiple countries to become territories and colonies to Great Britain, deemed to live under British rule. Through this, a multitude of violent crimes were committed to re-establish and maintain the empire.

The British Empire grew mighty on stealing jewels, cultural and historic items, land and people from over a quarter of the world for hundreds of years, which has allowed the royal family of the British monarchy system to live in luxurious wealth (Ringrose, 2022).

These crimes, which were committed through the agency of imperial wars and upheld through slavery and colonialism, have been legitimised through the upholstery of perceived British values and national identity via propaganda. The sanitisation of British Empire crimes that were endorsed by the British monarchy is a prime example of how this history has been destigmatised and chastised.

Under King George VI, the Bengal famine in India, the 'Jewel of the British Crown', killed over 4.5 million people. As a result of the 1952 Mau Mau uprising in Kenya, a demonstration resisting empire and colonialism, roughly 1.5 million people were forced into concentration camps where they were subjected to torture, rape and other violations. In West African and Caribbean Commonwealth nations, it is estimated that between 1640 and 1807 the British transported over

3.1 million Africans as cargo between colonies in the transatlantic slave trade. Many post–slave trade colonial projects continued to involve cocoa, sugar and tea industries that have enabled the royal family and British brands to have profited in billions up until the present day.

In the case of imperialism, many parts of the empire also provided men trained to kill: Ghanaians invaded German Togoland, West Indians crossed the border from Sierra Leone into German Cameroon, and Jews from soon-to-be-British Palestine (Jackson, 2008). Imperial control continued deep into Queen Elizabeth I's reign, which saw propaganda used as a tool to call people from the Commonwealth to 'the motherland' Great Britain, following the Second World War.

Today, British companies control more than $1 trillion worth of Africa's key resources and the Commonwealth. Today, many Commonwealth nations, including Jamaica and Barbados, demand reparations for the resource theft that occurred throughout the reign of the British monarchy on their land.

The royal family's wealth has been estimated at $28bn; Queen Elizabeth II never acknowledged or apologised for the atrocities of colonialism (Lawrence, 2022).

Empire propaganda as an imperialist tool

Propaganda was frequently used to boost the British Empire and efforts to colonise nations by promoting imperial wars ('Justice' by the *London Charivari*) and advertising the advantages of the British Empire through the exoticism of commercial goods ('Lipton Teas' by the *Illustrated London News*).

Throughout centuries, propaganda has sold the concept of empire to the British public as an essential part of British identity and patriotism. It has also provided the perfect opportunity to demonstrate racist stereotypes, to support the villainy of opposing powers to the legacy of the empire. Discover Society (2018) states that late 19th-century propaganda examples often included the composition of "the corrupt rajah, the ludicrous Chinese or Japanese nobleman, the barbarous 'fuzzy wuzzy' or black" against a heroic British officer.

Imperial propaganda of the late 19th and early 20th centuries was often found in music halls and theatres, school textbooks, biscuit tins and the marketing of popular brands including Lipton, Boy Scouts and Girl Guides and played a vital role in supporting Churchill's central role in the Bengal famine.

Companies which used propaganda strategy in their marketing were advocating not only for the consumerism of goods that were deemed 'exotic', but also for the exploitative systems in which they were produced. Through the promotion of tea, chocolate and tobacco, consumers were encouraged to normalise the necessity of the British Empire and unimagine a world without one.

In 2016, the political campaigns for Brexit demonstrated a resurgence of British Empire propaganda, as statements including "we can survive and thrive as never before" and "gives us the chance to start thinking globally and, by the way, bringing prices down for consumers" encouraged the British public to consider leaving the EU.

Empire propaganda continues to be a political source that defines the climate of xenophobia, white supremacy and racism, particularly the concept of racial purity in Great Britain (Hafiz, Discover Society, 2018).

Key words and phrases

Monarch – A sovereign leader of a state, including a king or emperor.
Monarchy – A form of government with a monarch as a lead.
Empire – An extensively large group of states or countries that are controlled by a superior power. *For centuries, the British Empire was controlled by the British monarchy.*

Colonialism – The practice of taking political control over another country, occupying it with settlers and exploiting its resources for economic gain.

Subjects – A person or thing that is being discussed or dealt with.

Lesson objective – To identify

Commonwealth – Countries that belonged to the British Empire.

Imperialism – A policy of extending a country's power and influence through diplomacy or military force.

Teacher resource guide

Propaganda examples:

● **The Spanish Armada portrait of Elizabeth I**

The Spanish Armada portrait of Elizabeth I is a portrait of Elizabeth I, the last Tudor queen with various symbols depicting the plot and defeat of the Spanish Armada, the instigation and expansion of the British Empire as a whole. Symbols to consider might be:

- her hand on the globe to demonstrate sovereignty, empire and dominance. Her fingers are resting on the Americas, to illustrate the ambitions of the British monarchy to instigate and sustain empire in this part of the world
- the contrasting scenes of the ships in the window behind her to demonstrate the war between England and Spain, known as the Spanish Armada
- the crown on her right-hand side to showcase her royal status
- pearls to symbolise her purity also implicate colonialism, as many historians believe that they were probably from Venezuela (Heyam, 2020)

● **James Gillray (1756–1815), 'The Plumb-pudding in Danger', 1805, London, Hand-coloured etching on paper, H 26.1 x W 36.3 cm © The Trustees of the British Museum**

'The Plumb-pudding [sic] in danger' is one of Gillray's most famous satires dealing with the Napoleonic wars in the early 19th century. British Prime Minister William Pitt sits on the left of the picture opposite Napoleon Bonaparte, both of whom tear hungrily at the globe in a bid to gain a larger portion. Though the intention of the piece is simple (by lampooning the avaricious pursuit of international dominance by both the French and British governments), Gillray's grotesque portrayal of the characters suddenly brings the cartoon alive. Note particularly the exaggeration of Pitt's skinny physique and Napoleon's beak-like nose: comical devices that would have quickly identified the subjects to his audience by appealing to popular conceptions of the two men.

By the British Library

● 'Our Allies, the Colonies' (RCMS 22/57/1)

British propaganda poster from the Second World War, printed in England by A.C. Ltd

Shows a Black soldier assuming his duties for the Second World War, wearing associated colours to Great Britain.

In-class lessons

Differentiation guide: *The activities will be differentiated by outcome. The listening and speaking part of today's lesson should encourage reflection and collaboration among a dynamic group of learners.*

Starter

See, think wonder: Analysis and discussion of messages through imagery.
   Turn off the lights and project the following images to the pupils. Display twice.

- **The Armada Portrait of Elizabeth I**
- **'The Plumb-pudding in danger' (1805) by James Gillray**
- **'Our Allies, The Colonies', Second World War poster**

During the first look, encourage pupils to observe the images in silence. Pause for about 5–10 seconds on each slide.
   During the second look, encourage pupils to discuss what they see, what they think, and what they wonder about the images.

Deeper questioning

1. What do you think these images have in common?
2. How do you think these images were used?
3. What impact could these images have on our lives today?

Encourage a student or assistant teacher to record the responses that the pupils have made. This could be via electronic device or scribing onto a working wall. You can use these responses at a later date to scaffold the detail of opinions that your pupils can offer this topic.

Explain to pupils that all three images are examples of *propaganda*

Ask pupils in partners to come up with their own definition of what they think that means.
   Next: Can they find the meaning of propaganda in a dictionary? Does it meet their expectations?
   Using a whiteboard, draw a word web of the following words: **propaganda**, **colonialism** and **empire**. Can pupils try to guess what the relationship between these three words are? Make a note of their responses, and explain that we will be investigating and debating the impact of these terms over time.

Activity guide

7–8

Instagram Ideas (Figure 17.1)

Pupils can create caption ideas for the Armada portrait of Elizabeth I included on the sheet.
Guiding questions: What can they see and how do they think she wants to present herself?
   What was the purpose of this image?

8–9 (Figure 17.2)

The story behind the image

'The Plumb-pudding in danger' (1805) by James Gillray

Pupils can use their inference skills to analyse 'The Plumb-pudding in danger' (1805) by James Gillray and draw a comic strip of the events that led to the making of this illustration.

9–11 (Figure 17.3)

Deeper inquiry

Reintroduce the three images from the starter to pupils:

The Armada Portrait of Elizabeth I, 'The Plumb-pudding in danger' (1805) by James Gillray, 'Our Allies, The Colonies', Second World War poster

Pupils can try to highlight as many historical vocabulary words as possible from the images, *including their titles*. In pairs, they can try to create a mini glossary of the terms using an Oxford Dictionary or a class iPad to research them.

Closing: 'British Things' by Horrible Histories, BBC

Pupils can share their discoveries from this video and come up with five questions about the British Empire that they want to investigate.

Further exploration ideas

National Curriculum links: Fairtrade (Geography), Percentages involving Statistics (Maths), World History, Informational and Persuasive Writing (English), Internet research (Computing)

1. *The big debate*

Pupils could continue using their research and speaking and listening skills to debate the following question:

"Should the monarchy be abolished?"

2. *The cost of chocolate*

Pupils could study the history of the relationship between the British monarchy and Ghana (formerly known as the Gold Coast) and how the cocoa industry fuelled the economic stability of the empire. A possible learning outcome idea could include a documentary (iMovie), PowerPoint presentation or information booklet published collectively by the class.

3. *Media campaign*

Pupils could use this Lipton's Tea advertisement from the early 20th century to consider how propaganda sometimes appears in subtle forms. Pupils could study British brands such as Lipton, Cadbury, Shell and BP to consider their relationship to the British Empire and how the monarchy has benefitted from such industries. A possible learning outcome could involve a digital media campaign that decleanses these traditional advertisements, and instead brings awareness to how these products have become a part of British society and culture.

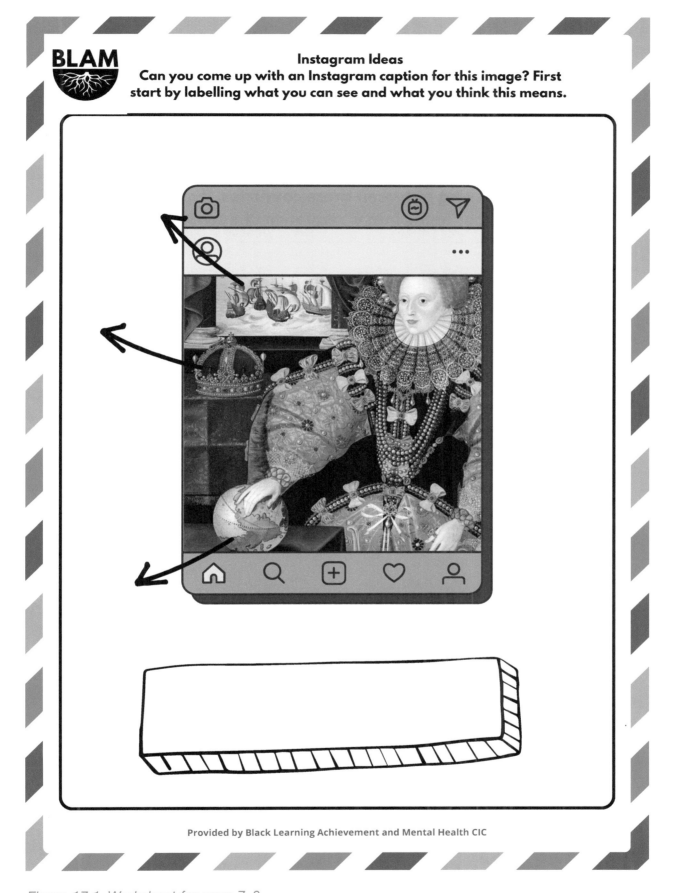

Provided by Black Learning Achievement and Mental Health CIC

Figure 17.1 Worksheet for ages 7–8

WASU Crossword

Answer the questions below by filling in the blanks in the puzzle.

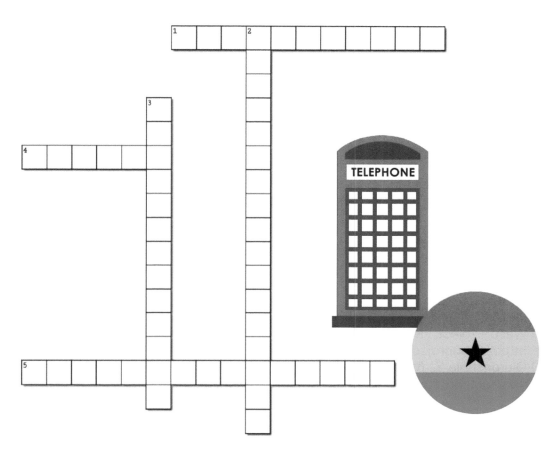

ACROSS

1. In London, some historical buildings have this. The WASU building does not have this
4. This is the continent Ladipo Solanke came from
5. This was the main attraction at the 'Empire Exhibit'

DOWN

2. This exhibition took place in Wembley, London.
3. This person was a member of WASU, and Ghana's first president.

Figure 18.3 Worksheet for ages 9–11

Notes

1 Oluronshola Y., How the West African Students Union Drove the Anti-colonial Agenda in 20th Century London [website], Quartz Africa, 6 March 2021, https://qz.com/africa/1979035/how-west-african-students-in-london-fought-for-african-independence/, accessed 18 May 2021; WASU Project, History of WASU [website], (WASU Project, no date), http://wasuproject.org.uk/history-of-wasu/, accessed 18 May 2021.

2 WASU Project [website], (WASU Project, no date), http://wasuproject.org.uk/history-of-wasu/, accessed 18 May 2021.

3 Ibid.

4 Archives Hub, 'West African students union' [website], (Archives Hub, no date), https://archiveshub.jisc.ac.uk/search/archives/100082dc-a3cc-3d57-94f8-0e7c4aac4926?component=b2c1b521-b6dc-3d6b-9bb8-e9383802d966, accessed 21 May 2021.

5 Oluronshola Y., [website] (Quartz Africa, 6 March 2021), https://qz.com/africa/1979035/how-west-african-students-in-london-fought-for-african-independence/, accessed 18 May 2021.

6 Ibid.

7 Ibid.

8 Oluronshola Y., [website] (Quartz Africa, 6 March 2021), https://qz.com/africa/1979035/how-west-african-students-in-london-fought-for-african-independence/, accessed 18 May 2021.

9 Ibid.

10 Ibid.

11 Ibid.

12 Ibid.

13 Ibid.

14 Dotse D. Y., West African Students Union's indelible Nkrumah [online], 1 October 2009, www.pambazuka.org/pan-africanism/west-african-students-unions-indelible-nkrumah, accessed 25 May 2021.

15 Ibid.

16 Yao Dotse D., 'West African Student's Union's Indelible Nkrumah' [website], (Pambazuka News, 1 October 2009), www.pambazuka.org/pan-africanism/west-african-students-unions-indelible-nkrumah, accessed 25 May 2021.

17 Ibid.

18 Ibid.

19 Wasu Project, 'Key figures: Ladipo Solanke' [website], (WASU Project, 29 January 2012), http://wasuproject.org.uk/history-of-wasu/, accessed 18 May 2021.

20 Oluronshola Y., [website] (Quartz Africa, 6 March 2021), https://qz.com/africa/1979035/how-west-african-students-in-london-fought-for-african-independence/, accessed 18 May 2021.

Part Two: Black presence in Europe

This part aims to give a spotlight to those narratives. We'll look at the Négritude movement in France, the Afro-Surinamese community in the Netherlands, Afro-Spaniards and more.

19 The Negritude movement

Lesson Title: The Negritude movement

Lesson Aims:

1. To understand what the movement meant to people of African descent living in France/Europe at the time
2. To learn the following skills: analyse the past and the present, how the movement is similar to modern-day liberation movements, using art methods such as Afro-surrealism

National syllabus links

English:

1. Develop the habit of reading widely and often, for both pleasure and information.
2. Appreciate our rich and varied literary heritage.
3. Become competent in the arts of speaking and listening, making formal presentations, demonstrating to others and participating in debate.

History:

1. Understand historical concepts such as continuity and change, cause and consequence, similarity, difference and significance; use them to make connections, draw contrasts, analyse trends and frame historically valid questions; and create their own structured accounts, including written narratives and analyses.
2. Gain historical perspective by placing their growing knowledge into different contexts, understanding the connections between local, regional, national and international history; between cultural, economic, military, political, religious and social history; and between short- and long-term timescales.

DOI: 10.4324/9781003194378-20

Art:

1. Produce creative work, exploring their ideas and recording their experiences.
2. Become proficient in drawing, painting, sculpture and other art, craft and design techniques.
3. Evaluate and analyse creative works using the language of art, craft and design.
4. Know about great artists, craft makers and designers, and understand the historical and cultural development of their art forms.

Worksheet Colour Code: Green: 7–8 Blue: 8–9 Orange: 9–11
Further outcomes for children: children's thinking skills and personal capabilities will be developed through opportunities for:

- Sharing opinions and engaging in group discussion (working with others)
- Reviewing research and coming to a conclusion (managing information)
- Organising and carrying out tasks (self-management)
- Developing listening and reflecting skills
- Public speaking through presentations of their work

The plenary

The Negritude movement was started by French-speaking African and Caribbean writers in the 1930s who were against French colonial rule and the negative effect it was having on people of African descent living in Africa and the Caribbean and across the greater African diaspora.

The movement was inspired by the Harlem Renaissance in the USA during the 1920s. There was a mass migration of African-Americans from the south of America which was heavily segregated to the north, due to the high levels of racial terror Black people faced in the segregated south. Once in the north, Black writers, artists and musicians took this more liberal stage and began to express their culture and experiences within their pieces more than ever before. Key figures of the Harlem Renaissance were people such as Langston Hughes – an American poet writing in segregated America, Claude McKay – Jamaican poet, and Louis Armstrong – Jazz musician. Both these movements, in the USA and France, occurred with the increase in 'Black Consciousness', a term that is used to define the recognition, awareness and in-depth understanding amongst Black people/persons of the oppressive realities imposed upon us as Black people globally. It is important to note that arising to make a stance for Black rights at this time required much resilience from its pioneers and the societies as structurally there were many obstacles put in place that would not allow African culture to flourish.

The founding fathers of Negritude

Leopold Senghor was born in Senegal –then a French colony – and moved to France, where he went to school. While in France, Senghor met Aime Cesaire. Cesaire was born in Martinique, a French colonial island in the Caribbean, in 1913. Cesaire was very keen in keeping in touch with his African heritage and would consider himself of Nigerian descent. He gained a scholarship to a prestigious school in Paris.

This is where he also met Leon Damas. Leon Damas was born in Guiana, which is another Caribbean island that was under French colonial rule in 1912, and he moved to France in 1929 to attend university.

Baker's first job was at a refugee centre. There, she welcomed those who had fled from the Nazi occupation of Belgium, as well as sought out and identified spies. It was Baker's connections and revered status which allowed her to frequent diplomatic functions – she was able to collect sensitive information about the movement of German troops and activities, as no one would suspect her. Baker wrote intelligence on her arms and hands and even pinned notes to the inside of her underwear.

However, the Nazis detected Josephine's resistance activity and visited her at her estate. The Nazis questioned her, but Baker was able to charm herself out of a situation which would have proven fatal. After this experience, Baker felt she could no longer stay in France. She was instructed to travel to London through Portugal[9] with Abtey. Both Abtey and Baker carried with them secret intelligence and classified documents. Baker wrote down the information she had with invisible ink on her sheet music.

In 1944, Paris was liberated and Baker returned to Paris in military uniform, having been heavily decorated by General de Gaulle due to her crucial contributions to French resistance.

Baker and the fight for civil rights in the US

Despite France being Baker's adopted home, she never truly turned her back on the US or the plight of Black people there. She often travelled back to the US to perform, tackled segregation directly and refused to perform to segregated audiences, even in the Jim Crow South. She was the first to dismantle colour lines and desegregate Las Vegas casinos. However, given the racist climate of the US, her fame did not shield her from racism in the same way that it did in France. In 1951 she was repeatedly refused admission to hotels and could not eat at restaurants. Whilst in New York, she made charges of racism to the police in response to the racist owner of a club who refused to serve her. Consequently, she was placed on the FBI 'watch list' and lost her US citizenship rights for a decade[10].

Baker would return to the US in 1963 with the aid of attorney general Robert F Kennedy. She arrived to speak at the March on Washington in her French air force uniform. As part of her speech she said:

> You know I have always taken the rocky path . . . I never took the easy one, but as I get older, and as I knew I had the power and the strength, I took that rocky path and I tried to smooth it out a little. I wanted to make it easier for you. I want you to have a chance at what I had.[11]

Later years

Baker continued to be a part of the movement, although many felt that she was out of touch and didn't feel that her efforts abroad contributed to the struggle for Black civil rights at home. In the late 60s, her health deteriorated and she struggled financially. Baker hoped to show that all people could live in harmony regardless of race or creed, and thus she adopted orphans from across the world to create her 'rainbow tribe'. However, she could not afford to support them all and fell into debt, unable to get out of it regardless of how hard she worked, leading her to lose her South of France chateau. In 1968, she played four sold-out shows in Carnegie hall at 68 years old before returning to the stage 18 months later to perform for the last time. The next night she died in her sleep of a stroke, and Baker received a military funeral with thousands attending to pay their respects[12].

References

Caravantes P., *The Many faces of Josephine Baker: Dancer, Singer, Activist, Spy*, 1st edn., Chicago, Chicago Review Press, 2015.

De Burton K., Siren of the Resistance: The Artistry and Espionage of Josephine Baker [website], 2021, www.nationalww2museum.org/war/articles/siren-resistance-artistry-and-espionage-josephine-baker, accessed 15 May 2021.

Griffith J., The It Girl: Josephine Baker: From Exotic Dancer to Activist [website], 2014, http://ww.bbc.com/culture/article/20141222-from-exotic-dancer-to-activist, accessed 15 May 2021.

Josephine Baker: The 1st Black Superstar [online video], Josephine Baker Tube, 13 November 2011, http://youtu.be/Ggb_wGTvZoU, accessed 15 May 2021.

Learning objectives	1. To understand the impact of Baker's role in the French resistance against the Nazis. 2. To understand Baker's involvement in the US civil rights movement and what she was able to achieve.
Main activities	1. PowerPoint/pamphlet 2. Video 3. Worksheets
Homework	1. Create a title page and/or a poem on the life of Josephine Baker.

In-class lessons

1. Create a slideshow which explains who Josephine Baker was, including her endeavours as a performer and her work as a spy.
2. Show the children the video listed in the teacher resource guide. Ask them to jot down their thoughts about the performance in pairs, and then feed this back to the class.
3. Complete relevant worksheets.

Key words and phrases

Nazi – A member of the National Socialist German Party.

Counterintelligence – Activities undertaken to prevent the spying of enemies.

Mein Kampf ('My Struggle') – Hitler's 1925 manifesto.

Chateau – French country house.

Rainbow Tribe – A group of children adopted by Baker from around the world, in an attempt to promote diversity and unity.

Resistance – Resistance within the Black and radical context, is a powerful and unyielding force that emerges as a response to systemic oppression, racism, and injustice. It represents a collective struggle for liberation, equality, and self-determination, often rooted in the historical experiences of Black communities. This resistance takes various forms, from grassroots activism to cultural expressions, aiming to dismantle oppressive structures, challenge the status quo, and reclaim the agency and humanity that have been denied for generations.

The plenary

Josephine Baker was an actress, performer and subsequent political activist and spy in her later years. At the height of her fame, she was revered and is remembered as the most famous music hall entertainer in France of all time. She reflected the beauty of African-American culture at the time and was a true trailblazer.

Further guide of future lessons:

1. The African diaspora in France.

Josephine Baker

Look at the pictures below. How do these places, things and animals relate to Josephine? Write below

France

_____
_____
_____
_____
_____
_____

Performing arts

_____
_____
_____
_____
_____
_____

Rainbow Tribe

_____
_____
_____
_____
_____
_____

Cheetah

_____
_____
_____
_____
_____
_____

Figure 20.1 Worksheet for ages 7–8

COMIC STRIP: A HISTORY OF AFRO-SPANIARDS

Figure 21.8 Worksheet for ages 8–9

BLAM

Afro-Spaniards - Zryab

Read and answer the questions below!

✳ What is Zryab famous for?

_____

✳ in what year did Zryab arrive in Spain. Once there, what did he become known for?

_____

_____

✳ Which common instrument of the time did he play, and what made his playing different?

_____

_____

✳ List some things we have today which were created by Zryab

_____

_____

_____

Figure 21.9 Worksheet for ages 9–11

22 Afro-Surinamese people in the Netherlands

Lesson Title: Afro-Surinamese people in the Netherlands

Lesson Aims:

To understand Afro-Surinamese communities in Europe

To learn about cultural customs the Afro-Surinamese people

To understand the historical and colonial ties of the Netherlands to Suriname. To learn about Afro-Surinamese migration and culture in modern-day Netherlands.

National syllabus links

History:

Pupils should regularly address and sometimes devise historically valid questions about change, cause, similarity and difference, and significance.

Human geography:

This includes types of settlement and land use, economic activity including trade links, and the distribution of natural resources including energy, food, minerals and water.

Worksheet Colour Code: Green: 7–8 Blue: 8–9 Orange: 9–11

The plenary

Teacher resource guide

The Surinamese are an Afro-descendant ethnic group in the Netherlands. They began migrating to the Netherlands over 50 years ago, from the then Dutch Guiana. Many Afro-Surinamese speak Dutch fluently; this is because Suriname was formerly Dutch Guiana. It was seized and colonised by the Netherlands in 1667. It gained independence from the Netherlands in 1975.

Suriname was one of South America's smallest countries.

Country profile

Many of its people are descended from enslaved Africans. Other groups that make up the country include Indian and Javanese indentured labourers brought over by the Dutch to work in agriculture. There are also small pockets of the land, the indigenous peoples communities are the Kaliña (Carib), Lokono (Arawak), Trio (Tirio, Tareno) and Wayana. Most political parties in the country are ethnically based.

DOI: 10.4324/9781003194378-23

AFRO- SURINAMESE PEOPLE IN THE NETHERLANDS

PLEASE FILL IN THE BLANKS USING THE WORD BANK ON THE NEXT PAGE

THE AFRO- SURINAMESE PEOPLE HAVE A FESTIVAL CALLED THE _____ SUMMER FESTIVAL, WHICH HAS BEEN HELD SINCE _____. THE FESTIVAL IS FAMILY FRIENDLY, AND THOUGH _____ IS THE MAIN ATTRACTION, THERE IS ALSO _____, _____ WORKSHOPS, FOOD AND DRINK IN THE PARK

NOTES

_____
_____
_____
_____
_____
_____
_____
_____
_____
_____

Figure 22.2 (Continued)

Figure 22.2 (Continued)

Name _____   Class _____

AFRO- SURINAMESE PEOPLE IN THE NETHERLANDS

Please use the word bank on the second page to fill in the gaps.

The _____ people are an Afro- descendant ethnic group in the Netherlands. Many Afro- Surinamese speak _____ fluently and descend from enslaved _____. In Suriname, there are _____ communities who originally fled Dutch slave plantations and then liberated themselves. These Maroons created villages in the rainforest that were _____ allowing maintenance of a distinctive _____ based on their West African origins.

Mass _____ to the Netherlands for Afro- Surinamese people did not happen until the _____ , when Suriname was gaining _____ from the Netherlands.

Cultural dress for the Afro- Surinamese includes a dress called _____ , a headwrap called _____ and a traditional clothing for men called _____ . These are usually worn on special occasions, such as birthdays or _____ ; dance parties only for women dressed in this traditional wear.

Many Afro- Surinamese use _____ , an African derived religion as a form of mental health support and physical healing.

The Afro- Surinamese people have a festival called the _____ Summer Festival, which has been held since 1975. The festival is family friendly, and though music is the main attraction, there is also _____ , _____ workshops, food and drink in the park.

Figure 22.3 Worksheet for ages 9–11

Name   **Year**

BLACK PRESENCE IN FRANCE

What is a griot?

Griots play an important role in the c_ltu_al history in ____st Africa. They are storytellers, p_a_se singers, po_ts, or musicians.

The role is hereditary, this means that it is p_ssed down through g_en_rations

Can you give an example of a famous griot heir?

(Hint: She's a famous singer from Mali)

_____

Provided by Black Learning Achievement and Mental Health CIC

Figure 23.1 (Continued)

Name _____   **Year** _____

BLACK PRESENCE IN FRANCE

What Black cultures can be seen in France?

What are the ingredients in some Afro-French dishes

_____

Provided by Black Learning Achievement and Mental Health CIC

Figure 23.1 (Continued)

BLACK PRESENCE IN FRANCE

Name

Year

Name 5 countries that have Afro-French communities

_____

_____

_____

_____

_____

What is a banlieue?

_____

_____

_____

Provided by Black Learning Achievement and Mental Health CIC

Figure 23.2 Worksheet for ages 8–9

Name _____   **Year** _____

BLACK PRESENCE IN FRANCE

What is a griot?

Griots play an important role in the c_ltu_al history in ____st Africa. They are storytellers, p_a_se singers, po_ts, or musicians.

Can you give an example of a famous griot?

(Hint: She's a famous singer from Mali)

_____

Provided by Black Learning Achievement and Mental Health CIC

Figure 23.2 (Continued)

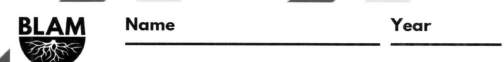

Name _____ **Year** _____

BLACK PRESENCE IN FRANCE

Write a spoken word piece in the style of a griot.

Use some of the creole words we have learnt today

_____

_____

_____

_____

_____

_____

_____

_____

_____

Provided by Black Learning Achievement and Mental Health CIC

Figure 23.2 (Continued)

BLAM

Name _____ **Year** _____

BLACK PRESENCE IN FRANCE

Name 5 countries that have Afro-French communities

_____

_____

_____

_____

_____

Explain the concept of 'Banlieues' and how they originated in France

_____

_____

_____

_____

_____

_____

_____

_____

_____

_____

Provided by Black Learning Achievement and Mental Health CIC

Figure 23.3 Worksheet for ages 9–11

Name _____   **Year** _____

BLACK PRESENCE IN FRANCE

What is a griot?

_____

_____

_____

_____

_____

Can you give an example of a famous griot heir?

_____

Provided by Black Learning Achievement and Mental Health CIC

Figure 23.3 (Continued)

Phillips N., 'Bristol bus boycott: Meet the faces behind the UK's own 1963 civil rights movement' [online], (Sky News, 12 October 2020), https://news.sky.com/story/bristol-bus-boycott-meet-the-faces-behind-the-uks-own-1963-civil-rights-movement-12086127, accessed 24 May 2022.

Pien D., 'British black panther party (1968–1973)' [online], (Black Past, 2 July 2018), www.blackpast.org/global-african-history/british-black-panther-party-1968-1973/, accessed 6 July 2021.

Pitts J., *Afropean: Notes from Black Europe*, Allen Lane, Penguin Books, 2019.

PsychoSean82, Skepta – That's Not Me (Clean) [online video], 9 June 2014, https://youtu.be/WRPDs2Q75lo, accessed 6 April 2021.

Rabaka R., *The Negritude Movement: W.E.B. Du Bois, Leon Damas, Aime Cesaire, Leopold Senghor, Frantz Fanon, and the Evolution of an Insurgent Idea*, Pennsylvania, Lexington Books, 2015.

Raleigh F., What Happened during the Bristol bus boycott?, Kaplan [online], www.kaplanpathways.com/about/news/what-happened-during-the-bristol-bus-boycott/, accessed 24 May 2022.

Richards E., 'Black British swing: Caribbean contribution to British Jazz in the 1930s and1940s' [online], (Black History Month, 1 February 2021), www.blackhistorymonth.org.uk/article/section/music-entertainers/black-british-swing-caribbean-contribution-to-british-jazz-in-the-1930s-and-1940s, accessed 6 April 2021.

Richards on Andrews C., 'The return of Jungle Fever brings together the best in old and new raving' [online], (The Guardian), www.theguardian.com/music/musicblog/2016/jul/22/return-jungle-fever-old-new-raving-20th-anniversary#:~:text=On%2023%20July%2C%20after%20a,Electric%20Brixton%20in%20south%20London, accessed 30 March 2022.

Roberts C., Discovering Black British Jazz, Arts and Humanities Research Council, https://ahrc.ukri.org/research/readwatchlisten/features/discoveringblackbritishjazz/, accessed 5 April 2021.

Safo K., and Wheeler S., 'The gentrification of Jungle' [online] (Mixmag, 23 October 2020), https://mixmag.net/feature/the-gentrification-of-jungle, accessed 8 April 2021.

Sayan Ghosh, Sayan Ghosh: History of Jungle Music (The Michigan Daily, 6 October 2019), www.michigandaily.com/section/arts/sayan-ghosh-history-jungle-music, accessed 8 April 2021.

Schwarz B., *West Indian Intellectuals in Britain*, 1st edn., Manchester, Manchester University Press, 2003, p. 50.

Shariatmadari D., 'What the Moors did for us' [website], (The Guardian, 31 January 2008), www.theguardian.com/artanddesign/artblog/2008/jan/31/itmayhavepassedyou, accessed 24 May 2021.

Sijlbing H. A., 'Jodensavanne, the Jerusalem on the river; A disputed heritage' (In: Balai L., and Schuster J.), *OSO: Magazine for Surinamese Linguistics, Literature and History DNBL* [magazine] 35 (2016), 71–82 (cited in Sibking, H. A., Institute for the Promotion of Surinamese Studies), www.caribheritage.org/events-opportunities/events/conferences/conference-paper/koto-and-angisa-conserving-creole-heritage

Simkin J., Stuart Hall [online], 2020, https://spartacus-educational.com/HIShallS.htm, accessed 25 April 2021.

Simpson H., 'The Jamaican short story: Oral and related influences', *Journal of Caribbean Literatures 4*(1) (2005), 11–30, www.jstor.org/stable/i40044340

Sky News, Fifty Years On: Read Enoch Powell divisive Rivers of Blood Speech, 20 April 2018, https://news.sky.com/story/fifty-years-since-enoch-powells-rivers-of-blood-speech-11338513, accessed 6 April 2021.

Smyth D., Black and Beautiful in Raphael Albert's Vintage Photographs of Beauty Contests (1854), 13 June 2008, www.1854.photography/2018/06/black-beautiful-albert/, accessed 5 July 2021.

Soetan L., 'Concept of naming in Yoruba culture', (Ekimogun Descendant, no date), www.ekimogundescendant.org/concept-of-naming-in-yoruba-culture/, accessed 29 June 2021.

Spanish Dictionary, 'Spanish words of Arabic Origin' [website], (Spanish Dictionary, n.d.), www.spanishdict.com/guide/Spanish-words-of-arabic-origin, accessed 26 May 2021.

Spanish Fiestas, 'History of Moorish Spain' [website], (Spanish Fiestas, n.d.), www.spanish-fiestas.com/history/Moorish-spain/, accessed 29 May 2021.

Spanish grammar articles and lessons, 'Spanish Dictionary', (no date), https://www.spanishdict.com/guide/spanish-words-of-arabic-origin, accessed 07 August 2023.

Spondonman, Oh Daddy! [1935] [online video], 21 September 2014, https://youtu.be/28cSAvvGwlY, accessed 5 April 2021 (Time stamp: 10:57–11:15)

Storrs L. R. Y., 'McCarthyism and the second Red Scare' [online], (Oxford Research Encyclopaedia of American History, 2015), https://doi.org/10.1093/acrefore/9780199329175.013.6, accessed 8 March 2022.

The Daily Show with Trevor Noah The Reparations Debate: Should America Compensate the Descendants of Slaves? | The Daily Show [online video], 22 March 2019, www.youtube.com/watch?v=3Uf_XDFXvzU, accessed 20 May 2022.

The Diet Blogger, 'The choice between Bitter Kola or Kola nut?', (Diet 234, no date), https://diet234.com/bitter-kola-kola-nut/, accessed 29 June 2021

The Editorial Team of the Tate Museum, 'Négritude' [website], (Tate, n.d.), www.tate.org.uk/art/art-terms/n/negritude#:~:text=N%C3%A9gritude%20was%20lead%20by%20the,surrealism%20and%20the%20Harlem%20Renaissance, accessed 25 January 2021.

The Editors of Encyclopedia Britannica, 'Hindu-Arabic numerals' [website], (Britannica, 9 September 2017), www.britannica.com/topic.Hindu-Arabic -Numerals, accessed 25 May 2021.

The Editors of Encyclopedia Britannica, 'Yoruba: People', (Britannica, 20 July 1998), www.britannica.com/topic/Yoruba, accessed 5 July 2021.

The Great In-between, From the Concrete Jungle to the Urban Jungle: The UK Junglist Massive Medium [online], 24 October 2014, https://medium.com/@thegreatinbetween/from-the-concrete-jungle-to-the-urban-jungle-the-uk-junglist-massive-14cc17f4be1b, accessed 28 March 2021.

The Joe Harriott Quintet-Topic, moanin [online video], 11 November 2014, https://youtu.be/Cq_fpsoMGX0, accessed 7 April 2021.

The Muslim Heritage Editorial Team, 'Ziryab, the Musician, Astronomer, Fashion Designer and Gastronome' [website], (Muslim Heritage, 13 June 2003), http://muslimheritage.com/ziryab-the-musician/

The Price Academy, Black Tudors: Who was Dederi Jaquoah? Learn more on The Prince of the River Cestos! [online video], 4 August 2020, https://youtu.be/c4PBLDJo7wE, accessed 18 April 2021.

The Price Academy, Black Tudors: Who was Jacques Frances? Henry 8th Salvage Diver for the Mary Rose [online video], The Price Academy, 28 June 2020, http://youtu.be/T1PJ9SgC4U8, accessed 18 April 2021.

The Price Academy, Black Tudors: Who was John Blanke? Learn More on the Amazing Story of the Tudor Trumpeter! [online video], The Price Academy, 25 June 2020, http://youtu.be/JfTaXRFV7EA, accessed 18 April 2021.

The Price Academy, Black Tudors: Who was Mary Fillis? Learn More on the Moroccan Seamstress who Changed Faiths! [online video], The Price Academy, 30 June 2020, http://youtu.be/C9Slpuizx5y, accessed 18 April 2021.

The Price Academy, Black Tudors: Who was Reasonable Blackman? Learn More on the Prosperous Black Tudor Silk Weaver! [online video], 20 July 2020, http://youtu.be/UObl4OUJiUw, accessed 18 April 2021.

Them Never Love, 'Mangrove Nine 1970's – Darcus Howe, Frank Crichlow, etc. . . .', 26 March 2012, www.youtube.com/watch?v=tQQLLtfNhcY&t=193s, accessed 24 May 2022.

Thomas D., *Black France*, Bloomington, IN, Indiana University Press, 2007.

Toasije A., 'The Africanity of Spain: Identity and problematization', *Journal of Black Studies 39*(3) (2009), 348–355, www.jstor.org/stable/40282566

Toasije, A., 'The Africanity of Spain: Identity and problematization', *Journal of Black Studies 39*(3) (2009), 348–355, https://doi.org/10.1177/0021934706297563.

Today in Focus, 'Revisited: How the Bristol bus boycott changed UK civil rights' [podcast], (The Guardian, 26 August 2020), www.theguardian.com/news/audio/2020/aug/26/revisited-how-the-bristol-bus-boycott-changed-uk-civil-rights-podcast, accessed 24 May 2022.

Todd J., Bringing the Untold Stories of Black Tudors into the Classroom, Oxford University, www.history.org.uk/files/download/21044/1558524345/SSJT4__Jason_Todd__Chris_Lewis__Bringing_the_untold_stories_of_black_Tudors_into_the_classroom.pdf, accessed 17 April 2021.

Toynbee J., Tackley C., and Doffman M., *Black British Jazz: Routes, Ownership and Performance*, 1st edn., Surrey, Ashgate Publishing Company, 2014, pp. 25–44.

Tucker J., This is Our Music: Rave, Race and Rhythm in the Jungle (Part 1/3), Halcyon Wax [online video], 27 July 2020, www.halcyonwax.com/post/this-is-our-music-rave-race-and-rhythm-in-the-jungle-part-1–3, accessed 29 March 2021.

van Andel T., and Westers P., 'Why Surinamese migrants in the Netherlands continue to use medicinal herbs from their home country', *Journal of Ethnopharmacology* (2010), 694–701, https://doi.org/10.1016/J.JEP.2009.11.033

Vauxhall History, 'Claudia Jones's Vauxhall years and the genesis of the West Indian Gazette' [online], (Vauxhall History, 6 April 2021), https://vauxhallhistory.org/claudia-jones, accessed 12 April 2021.

Walker R., 'Cultural revolutions: How Dub Reggae's Beats conquered 70's Britain' [online], (The Guardian, 27 September 2020), www.theguardian.com/music/2020/sep/27/soundtrack-of-a-city-how-dub-reggae-shook-and-shaped-london, accessed 24 May 2022.

WASU Project, 'History of WASU' [online], (WASU Project, no date), http://wasuproject.org.uk/history-of-wasu/, accessed 18 May 2021.

WASU Project, 'Key figures: Ladipo Solanke' [online], (WASU Project, 29 January 2012), http://wasuproject.org.uk/history-of-wasu/ accessed 18 May 2021.

Watts R., 'Negritude, présence africaine, race', In *Postcolonial thought in the French Speaking World*, edited by C. Forsdick and D. Murphy, 1st edn., Liverpool, Liverpool University Press, 2009, https://www.jstor.org/stable/j.ctt5vjgn6.22

'Why the future of France is African' [website], (BBC World News, 8 April 2019), www.bbc.co.uk/news/world-africa-47790128

Williams D., Yoruba Naming Ceremony Part 1 [online video], 31 January 2017, https://youtu.be/dohzZvp-Dlo, accessed 29 June 2021.

Williams D. R., 'Stress and the mental health of populations of color: Advancing our understanding of race-related stressors', *Journal of Health and Social Behavior 59*(4) (2018), 466–485, https://doi.org/10.1177/0022146518814251

Winston T., Winston Trew [online], 1 March 2020, www.brh.org.uk/site/contributors/winston-trew/, accessed 6 July 2021.

Witness History, The Bristol bus boycott [online video], BBC, 10 October 2019, www.bbc.co.uk/programmes/w3csyx08, accessed 24 May 2022.

Yan'kyaa L., 'Eric and Jessica Huntley' [online], (Black History Month, 5 February 2019), www.blackhistorymonth.org.uk/article/gallery/test-diane-julie-abbott-politician/, accessed 29 June 2021.

Younis J., 'The art of resistance', (Lawrence Wishart, 3 February 2021), http://lwbooks.co.uk/the-art-of-resistance, accessed 16 April 2021.

Ziryab, poet of Cordoba, 'Cities of light', (2020), http://www.islamicspain.tv/arts-and-literature/ziryab-poet-of-cordoba, accessed 07 August 2023.